Yesterday's Indiana

Seemann's Historic States Series

BYRON L. TROYER

Yesterday's
INDIANA

Seemann's Historic States Series No. 4

E. A. Seemann Publishing, Inc.
Miami, Florida

WITHOUT THE HELP of many Hoosiers and those from other states, this book would not have been possible. The many valuable contributions of individuals, businesses, and institutions are gratefully acknowledged (in abbreviated form) at the end of each caption. All pictures without source indication in the caption come from the author's own collection.

Adams	Mrs. John Q. Adams, Columbia City	Long	Judith R. Long, Salt Lake City, Utah
Allen	J. C. Allen & Son, West Lafayette	National	National Gypsum Company,
Bone	Perry K. Bone, Arcadia, Florida	Gypsum	Buffalo, New York
DePauw	DePauw University Archives, Green-castle	News	*Indianapolis News*
ECC	Evansville Chamber of Commerce	NIHS	Northern Indiana Historical Society, South Bend
EVC	*Evansville Courier*	Notre Dame	Notre Dame du Lac University, South Bend
FBH	Fort Benjamin Harrison		
FMNB	First Merchants National Bank of Michigan City	Pulliam	Eugene S. Pulliam, Indianapolis
		Purdue	Purdue University, West Lafayette
FWHS	Allen County-Fort Wayne Historical Society	Purdue Ag.	Purdue Agricultural Experiment Station, West Lafayette
FWPL	Fort Wayne Public Library	Richter	Harold Richter, Rockville
GP-T	*Gary Post-Times*	SMA	St. Meinrad Academy
Goodpasture	William Goodpasture, Canaan	Schwomeyer	Herbert F. Schwomeyer, Indianapolis
Hanover	Hanover College	Sheraton	French Lick-Sheraton Hotel
Harper's	*Harper's Magazine*	Speedway	Indianapolis Speedway, Indianapolis
Heinz	H. J. Heinz Company, Pittsburgh, Pennsylvania	Standard	Standard Oil Company of Indiana, Chicago, Illinois
Hohenberger	Frank Hohenberger, Nashville	USS	United States Steel Corporation, Gary
Hudson	Jerry C. Hudson, Sr., Goshen		
Huntington	Huntington College	VCHS	Vigo County Historical Society, Terre Haute
ISL	Indiana State Library, Indianapolis		
ISU	Indiana State University, Terre Haute	VU	Vincennes University, Lewis Historical Library
LPHS	La Porte County Historical Society	Wilcox	Sandy Wilcox, North Fort Myers, Florida
Leslie's	*Leslie's Pictorial History*		
Lilly	Lilly Library, Indiana University, Bloomington	WLBC	Winona Lake Bible Conference
		Woodson	Weldon D. Woodson, Alhambra, California
Lockridge	Ross Lockridge, Bloomington		
Lockwood	George Lockwood, Muncie	Woodworth	Woodworth Photos, Fort Wayne

Library of Congress Cataloging in Publication Data

Troyer, Byron L
    Yesterday's Indiana.

    (Seemann's historic states series ; no. 4)
    SUMMARY: Brief text and numerous historical photo-graphs, engravings, drawings, woodcuts, etc., trace Indiana's history from first settlement to the early 1950's.
    1. Indiana--History--Pictorial works. 2. Indiana--Description and travel--Views. [1. Indiana--History--Pictorial works. 2. Indiana--Description and travel--Views] I. Title.
F527.T76   977.2'0022'2   75-14381
ISBN 0-912458-55-0

Manufactured in the United States of America by Paragon Press, Montgomery, Alabama

To

Iona Troyer

for her valued help and support

Contents

Foreword

THE TASK of presenting a pictorial history of Indiana and its people in "Seemann's Historic States Series" has been a challenging one. The format is is nearly unique in books about Indiana and the wedding of text and photographs I found a most happy pattern. This book is not meant to be an exhaustive, complete exercise in historical scholarship, but rather a presentation of the state's history in pictures that are rarely accessible to the average individual.

The time-worn cliche that "one picture is worth a thousand words" may be an exaggeration, but it is certainly true that a photo or engraving presents an almost instant, accurate image of a steamboat, a native of Brown County, or a horse streetcar. Hundreds of words of text could not accomplish that.

Anyone who becomes seriously involved in writing popular history soon must realize that it is impossible to write the whole truth, the exact truth. Six sources for an event of long ago may give six versions, varying greatly. Then one must make a judgment, choosing that which seems most reliable. Records left by self-serving "heroes," political propagandists, incompetents, and people with very faulty or faded memories or strong biases are additional factors.

These frustrations led a cynical historian to declare that "history is the lies we all agree on."

But the camera never lies. It may not tell the whole story, but what it tells is true. Photos show details and atmosphere the writer can only awkwardly hint at, despite many words.

I found early, as an ambitious young free-lancer for magazines, that it was almost imperative to include suitable photos or other illustrations to sell nonfiction manuscripts. Since nearly one-third of the illustrations in this book are photos taken by myself or are the work of others preserved in my files over the years, I wish I could remember and have space to thank all those who have helped me with photography and photo-editing.

Starting as a teen-ager with a 3-A Kodak, I was most fortunate to have the guidance of Ben Larrimer, of Marion. He had been associated with Alfred Steichen in demonstrating that photography could be a creative art. News photography was in its infancy—so much so that most daily newspapers had neither a darkroom nor a full-time photographer. Later, John Logan, also of Marion, was unstinting with help from a vast all-around camera experience.

Then came Life magazine. Photo-journalism came into its own. The great photo-journalists who contributed chapters of Morgan and Lester's "Graphic-Graflex Photography," along with scores of other photographers and photo-graphers and photo-editors have left me in their debt. More than that, they help me to an appreciation, which it is hoped my readers will share, of the invaluable records left by the old-time photographers with their slow lenses and antique equipment.

Unfortunately, most of these early cameramen cannot be identified. However, special mention can be made of the Bass Photo Co. of Indianapolis, which has graciously given permission for the use of many of its photos and negatives given by them to the Indiana State Library. Their photographic record of Indianapolis goes back to before the Civil War!

Another remarkable photographer whose work can be designated is Frank Hohenberger. He spent a long lifetime photographing Brown County and ad-joining areas. It is possible to present many of his pictures through the cour-tesy of the Josiah K. Lilly Library and the Indiana University Foundation which has granted permission to reproduce and publish them. Credited also are several pictures, when known, by J. C. Allen & Son of West Lafayette, Indiana, without doubt the best American farm photographers of this cen-tury.

Worthy of special note are the fine historical photograph collections of the Indiana State Library's Indiana Division, Fort Wayne Public Library, Allen County-Fort Wayne Historical Society, Northern Indiana Historical Society, and LaPorte Historical Society. Their directors, respectively, Mrs. Hazel Hop-per, Fred Reynolds, Gary Ernst, James Sullivan and Mrs. Madeline G. Kinney, and their staffs were unstinting with help in selecting and identifying material from their files.

After an extensive search, two serious vacuums remained—unthinkable when dealing with Indiana—namely photos of the state basketball champion teams and of several of the state's best-known and most flamboyant twen-tieth-century personalities. For the former, we are grateful for permission to use pictures from the remarkable collection of Herbert F. Schwomeyer, used in his book, "Hoosier Hysteria." For the latter Eugene S. Pulliam, publisher of Indianapolis Newspapers, Incorporated, came to the rescue with portraits of D. C. Stephenson, Dillinger, and others from the files of the *Indianapolis Star* and *Indianapolis News*.

Finally, I am grateful for the cooperation of many other institutions, public and private, and of individuals who aided me in various ways in the search for meaningful illustrations.

In addition to those listed in the photo acknowledgments, the following persons were particularly helpful: Arlene and Bob Apley, Elletsville; Craig J. Beardsley, Indianapolis; Al Bloemker, Indianapolis; Miss Boyd Bowers, Pittsburgh, Pennsylvania; Robert Cooper, LaFontaine; Albertha M. Jacob, Indianapolis; Thomas Krasean, Vincennes; Lenord U. Kreuger, Evansville; Virginia L. Mauck, Bloomington; Tom Philipson, South Bend; James E. Rasmussen, Gary; Bruce and Sue Troyer, Plainfield, and Phil Van Blaricum, Indianapolis. To many other archivists, not mentioned here, my heartfelt thanks.

Byron L. Troyer

Fort Myers, Florida, 1975

THE FIRST HOOSIERS: A Dr. Koch of St. Louis anticipated most archeologists by a century when he concluded in 1839 that man had existed in what is now Indiana ten to twelve thousand years ago during the last stages of the ice age. Hardy, primitive people pursued the mastodons and other now extinct animals, killing them as their principal food. This drawing appeared in William Cullen Bryant's popular U.S. history, published in 1881. It is now believed that these primitive people used short spears instead of bows, which had not yet been invented.

A HUNTER'S SPEAR POINT: The stone relic shown, known as the Folsom point, is the principal evidence left by primitive mastodon hunters in Indiana. (Eli Lilly)

THE BIRDSTONE is a rare prehistoric relic, seldom found outside Indiana. Patiently ground from granite, slate, or porphyry by crude means, birdstones show the artistic ability of prehistoric man. Their purpose is still unknown. (Eli Lilly)

Indiana from 10,000 B.C. to 1679

AN INHABITANT of Indiana, for any length of time, becomes a Hoosier. There is something in the soil, the climate, and the tradition that makes this inescapable. The Hoosier, in recent decades, has always been in the center of things. And if you want to go on any long trip across the continent, the chances are more than even that you will go through or over Indiana.

Nearly all the greatest inland trade and emigration routes since 1700 have passed through Indiana. The center of population of the United States for six straight decades until 1950 was in Indiana. Indianapolis, its capital, adopted the nickname, "Crossroads of America," because the old National Road, now Washington Street (U.S. 40, I-70), and the Old Michigan Road (U.S. 31), now Meridian Street, intersected there. With all the other great highways, water and surface and air, going through its boundaries, the entire state made the name its own.

This is an essential fact for non-Indianans, but it is equally vital for the Hoosier to know in order to understand himself and his state. Indiana, like "poor little Rhode Island," is a mighty midget. Few realize that Indiana is the smallest in area of all the contiguous thirty-seven states west of the Alleghenies. Although the heavens blessed it with a soil without peer, and an invigorating climate, its mineral resources are small.

From its earliest history, its greatest natural asset has been location, with the Great Lakes washing its northwest shore, and the Ohio River lapping its southern boundary. The lakes connect it through the Erie Canal and the St. Lawrence Seaway with the Atlantic at Montreal and New York, and give the state easy all-water access to giant iron, coal, and copper mines. Even the wheat from Western plains and Canada is shipped on this easy water route.

When the heavily populated East sent its emigrants west to the fertile plains or the goldfields, they found that the pioneer Indiana roads and railroads provided the most direct and best route. Many of these pioneers saw Indiana as the land of opportunity, and remained.

Hoosiers have claimed—and they are so regarded by many others—to be the most typical Americans. Its many well-known writers nurtured and promoted the image of a Hoosier as a native-born American, with stalwart, self-reliant, pioneer antecedents, and a homespun sense of humor. He had democratic qualities born of the soil not so evident in the class-society of the East.

There is some very good basis for this image. When Indiana was made a state in 1816, every white male in the state could vote, different from Massachusetts and all other states east of the mountains where laws confined the electorate to landowners, and disenfranchised three-fourths of the population. The Indiana constitution of 1850 was the first charter of any state to provide for universal free education. Although its pioneer schools were sadly deficient, the state soon forged to the front in education.

It has often been said that the term "Hoosier" is better known than any regional nickname of the United States, except Yankee. With it goes the Hoosier dialect, employed by many authors, especially Edward Eggleston and Kin Hubbard (Abe Martin). The dialect, the pioneer and rural background, and the rural wit and humor have given the name an image of the Hoosier as a rustic with a little sophistication and guile.

The Hoosier accepts this image proudly and good-naturedly for he knows, as has often been demonstrated, that outsiders have no advantage over him in a horse trade or a political campaign. The plain language and the homely humor played a great part in carrying one Hoosier, Abraham Lincoln, to the White House. Eastern professors and editors who had scoffed at the idea of this rustic western bumpkin in the White House, came to marvel at the simple eloquence of his prose. In his too-modest and too-brief autobiography, he stated simply that "I was raised in Indiana." Note, he did not say "reared;" that was not the language of a Hoosier.

In the pioneer days, the discipline of psychiatry had never been heard of. If a pioneer Hoosier appeared to be eccentric, a little "tetched," or had a streak of genius, it was attributed to having been kicked in the head by a horse as a youngster. His peers let it go at that. It is hard to say how the head shrinker would have disposed of them but, two such Hoosiers, Abraham Lincoln and Johnny Appleseed, achieved immortality.

Who was the first Hoosier? A Dr. Koch, of St. Louis, was a physician who knew little about medicine and less about archaeology, for both were infant sciences. He reported a remarkable find. He did know some geology, which Sir Charles Lyell was bringing out of its infancy, and became an ardent fossil collector. Among his finds was the skeleton of a mastodon which he dug out of the ground. Associated with it were large quantities of ashes and prehistoric weapon points and other artifacts, which indicated to him that man had killed, roasted, and eaten the giant beast.

His conclusion that man must have been present in the Midwest at the twilight of the Pleistocene era, the age of the great American glaciers, set off lively controversies. It was known that the Mastodon became extinct about that time. Professional archaeologists, led by the prestigious Dr. Alex Hrdlcka, steadfastly fought the doctor's theory until two decades ago. They doubted that primitive man could have crossed over the great ice sheets from Siberia. The overwhelming evidence of new finds as well as radioactive dating finally brought them to agree with Dr. Koch, that man, known as the Folsom man, was here at the close of the Pleistocene or approximately ten thousand to twelve thousand years ago.

They were exciting times in Indiana when the Folsom man appeared. The Wisconsin glacier was retreating an inch or so a year as the warming climate melted its edges. Through Northern and Central Indiana it left a series of gravelly moraine ridges interspersed with marshy plains. On these grazed herds of mastodons, woolly mammoths, now-extinct species of bison, camels, and horses. The bone-chilling melted waters of the ice rushed in raging rivers which drained the lakes formed at the edges of the two-thousand-foot deep ice. In them tumbled icebergs while along their bottoms rolled boulders, gravel and sand, cutting their way even through the bed limestone.

Geologists tell us that the generally-placid Wabash and its wide valley was once the principal outlet for what now are the Great Lakes. The great stream, over a mile wide and filled a hundred feet deep with raging water, dwarfed Niagara and the St. Lawrence of today.

Little can be said with certainty of the Folsom people, except that the evidence indicates they were a fierce, nomadic people. roaming continuously after big game. The land was rugged; the climate cruel. When they had found a mastodon, they cunningly used fire and fiendish yells to scare it into a marsh where it became mired. With exquisitely-flaked, thin spear-points, their spears were thrown at the beast until one pierced the rib cage and found a vital spot.

It was a dangerous task, attacking the enraged giant at close range, and many people surely were killed or crippled in the hunt. The Folsom people camped and gorged on the mastodon meat until it was gone or decomposed. Then, they all packed their meager possessions, man, woman, and child, and were off through the awful land in hunt of more prey.

Folsom man can certainly qualify as a Hoosier pioneer—courageous and resourceful. Perhaps he even ate the luscious "Hoosier Banana" (paw-paw) and drank sassafras tea, to vary his diet, just as tourists do in rustic Brown County today.

The Folsom man probably was the ancestor of the American Indian tribes of today. So, too, were succeeding primitive cultures, several of whom are known as "mound builders." Archaeologists divide them into four or five successive groups, whose artifacts indicate widely differing ways of life and customs. These are generally classified in order of age as Paleo, Archaic, Woodland, and Mississippian.

Gradually, after most of the grazing animals became extinct, the Folsom people took to hunting smaller game and gathering wild fruits and herbs. The latest indication was that the tribes began agriculture in Indiana quite late—about 2,000 years ago, although this date may be pushed back farther too. With agriculture and more settled villages, these early Indians could devote more time to religion and the arts. Pottery came into use; polished stone images were made for ornaments and religious use. The dog was domesticated. Corn, beans, and pumpkins became staple foods, not only in season but were preserved and stored for winter use along with dried berries.

Among prehistoric relics found in Indiana have been some of the finest prehistoric art north of the Rio Grande—beautiful steatite effigy pipes, which can be identified as to species of animal and birds; and long, thin obsidian lance heads. The Indians had developed trade and again, "all roads lead to Indiana." Among the Hopewell mounds which provided these artifacts were found marine shells from the Gulf, obsidian from Yellowstone, copper from Isle Royale, and mica from the southern Alleghenies.

When white explorers first reached Indiana, the Miami Indians, a branch of Algonquin group, were the principal tribe in addition to two or three related but smaller tribes. As the pioneers pushed back the Shawnees, Delawares, and Pottawattomies, who were all related, they came to Indiana to take refuge with the Miamis.

MESSAGES FOR ETERNITY were left by prehistoric Hoosiers—if we could only understand them! This Indian petroglyph (rock writing) collected by a Logansport man is in the collection of the Northern Indiana Historical Society at South Bend. (NIHS)

ABORIGINAL INDIANS left in their graves skeletons and a few time-defying personal possessions which enable archaeologists to piece together a sketchy story of their lives. (NIHS)

Indiana from 1679 to 1830

THE FIRST WHITE MEN to discover and occupy Indiana were the French, the most adventurous and intrepid of all the European explorers.

Mostly of Viking stock from the Norman part of France, they were spurred on by two great thirsts—one for wealth in the form of beaver pelts, the other, in the case of the missionaries, by a zeal to rescue the heathen from perdition.

These men were fur traders, explorers and woods rangers, one of whom may have reached Indiana as early as 1650. It is quite likely that he could have been some forgotten, unnamed outlaw who traded with the Indians without a license from King Louis XV. As this offense carried the death penalty, he would not be likely to leave records, and probably was an illiterate to begin with.

Father Jacques Marquette, a Jesuit priest from the mission in Mackinaw, Michigan, who had visited Indian villages on the Illinois River in 1673, met two such renegades at the site of present-day Chicago. He was desperately ill, and because the two, one of whom was a physician, nursed him through the winter of 1674, he charitably omitted their names in his journal.

While local historians in northwestern Indiana insist that Father Marquette was the first white man to set foot on what is now Indiana soil, historians generally agree that Robert Cavelier Sieur de la Salle, and a party of seventeen including three Recollect friars first arrived in Indiana in 1679 when they discovered the portage from the St. Joseph River to the Kankakee, at what is now South Bend. While la Salle, an affluent man of a noble family and his three Recollect associates were well-educated, the key figure in the party was an Indian guide, White Beaver. He was Mohican, who with a small band of his tribe's Wolf Clan had fled before the English and moved to the banks of the Kankakee, the name of which, originally Theakiki, derived from his tribe, translated as River of the Wolves.

ROBERT CAVALIER SIEUR de la Salle was the first white man definitely known to have set foot on Indiana soil. He and his party of fourteen reached present-day South Bend on December 3, 1679. (NIHS)

THIS BLAZED CEDAR, found in June 1897, is the oldest relic of white explorers in the state. Father Ribourde, a priest with la Salle, had axed a blaze mark in the tree to mark the portage path at the St. Joseph River—our first highway marker. (NIHS)

Following his discovery of the portage, laSalle returned the following year to the site and signed a treaty with the Miamis. In 1682, he used the same portage to make his historic voyage down to the mouth of the Mississippi River. La Salle was possibly the greatest of all our explorers, yet the exertions he demanded of his men were more than many of them could take, and the last attempt to assassinate him was successful in 1687.

The Miamis were a proud, able people whose traits caused the early French to call them superior to other tribes. But their pride was their greatest fault—and their love of war. They did not hesitate to fight the Iroquois and the Sioux who were equally fierce warriors but outnumbered them, even though they did not have guns, which the Iroquois did. The French later gave them guns and admonished them "to punish the Iroquois"—and the decimation of the Miamis went on, aided by occasional smallpox epidemics. The proud tribe finally fought desperately against domination by all the white powers, French British or American.

The dates of the first French settlements in Indiana are uncertain. But modern historians, to appease local pride, generally agree that the first permanent settlements were all started "about 1720" at present-day Fort Wayne (Kekionga), Lafayette (Ouiatenon), and Vincennes. For all practical purposes, the first settlement was about seven miles from South Bend, in the south edge of present-day Niles, Michigan. A mission was built there in 1687 where the Great Sauk Indian Trail connecting Detroit and Chicago intersected with the trail to the South Bend portage. A fort was constructed here about 1691 and remained headquarters for fur traders, missionaries, and soldiers for the entire region until the Revolution. The French, seeking to control a vast land—the entire Great Lakes and Mississippi River basins—with a few men, hoped to induce the Miamis and all the other Midwest tribes to locate their villages at Fort St. Joseph and Detroit.

But the Miamis rebelled at the plan and reverted to their traditional homes in the Wabash and Maumee valleys. Sieur de Vincennes the Elder tried vainly for twenty years to induce them to come to the strategic forts. So the new forts at Kekionga, Ouiatenon, and Vincennes were established with their surrounding hamlets.

The French inhabitants lived in an era of bloodshed and hardship. They performed incredible labor in the fur-bearing season and faced death at the hands of enemy and rebel Indians. But, in the summer, they did only enough farming to provide for their own needs and whiled away their spare time with gay parties.

All life revolved about the greedy lust for beaver skins, to be sent back to Europe where they would make warm robes and stylish hats for the high and the mighty. The mission of the French soldiers, traders, and settlers was to mobilize the tribesmen in the ceaseless quest for pelts. "Catch the beaver!

CHIEF AWTAWAWTAW of the Indiana Miamis, responsible for the great French and Indian War, became a martyr after he moved his tribesmen to this spot on the Miami River, near Piqua, Ohio. It is shown as it appeared in the early 1800s when occupied by the home of Col. John Johnston, government agent for Indiana and Ohio tribes.

Catch the beaver," the French exhorted the Indians. "Then, you can trade it for the superior white man's goods—the steel knife and the steel ax that cuts ten times as well. The brass hawk bells that will adorn your wrist and tinkle merrily when you jog down the trail! The white man's milk (fire water) which will make your belly warm and your troubles go away."

In the summer, flotillas of pirogues, fashioned out of hollowed logs, would take the rich haul of beaver skins, along with otter, deer, muskrat, and other skins to Montreal.

But the Indian, illiterate as he was, knew the difference between the three beaver pelts the French demanded for a pound of powder, and the two pelts the British traders asked. Trouble was brewing in Indiana—trouble that would make American history.

Greedy playboy king that he was, Louis XV of France took such exorbitant taxes from the fur trader's loot that they could not compete with the British on price.

The English were losing their timidity, thanks to some tough Scotch-Irishmen who were used to hardships. They had reached the far frontier of Pittsburgh in Pennsylvania early in the 1700s, and were engaged in the fur trade. Soon, they heard of the rich haul of furs to be had in Indiana and adjoining areas. They loaded their goods on pack horses and moved them the hard way through the raw wilderness of modern Ohio, following Indian trails. On the

Miami River, north of present Dayton, Ohio, they built a crude log fort and set up shop.

The Indians around Kekionga (Fort Wayne) were invited to trade and get big prices for the fur. Le Pied Froid (Cold Foot) was the man the French called head chief of the Miamis, and they had counted on him to keep the Indians in line. But a chief was not an all-powerful monarch as European explorers thought and many writers suggest today. His power came only from the council of sub-chiefs and warriors who elected him.

Awtawawtaw (The grane, La Demoiselle) was the real chief. He had helped Orontony (Nicolas), a Wyandot chief, who also thought the French were fleecing the Indians, in an abortive revolt in 1747. When Awtawawtaw suggested the tribe follow him to Pickawillany (Piqua) where the Scotch-Irish traders built their post on the Miami, all but three lodges deserted Le Pied Froid and went along.

In 1747, Celeron Sieur de Bienville made his historic voyage down the Ohio and back to the Great Lakes with a small army. He warned the British that the French owned the Ohio country, all the way to Pittsburgh, by the right of laSalle's discoveries and French occupation. He gave an ultimatum to Awtawawtaw and his Miami nation to move back to Kekionga or else. He ordered the British traders to return to Pennsylvania.

Awtawawtaw was a diplomat—"Onontio (father) we can't leave now, the corn is not ready for harvest. We will come in the winter after the harvest." Bienville was skeptical but agreed. But Awtawawtaw never kept his promise. Great history, generally unknown to Americans, was made at Pickawillany.

The Miamis of Indiana were party to the opening battle of the frontier holocaust on June 21, 1752 that grew into the eleven-year French and Indian War. The unsung Miami Indian, who knew when the French were cheating him in the beaver trade, was the martyr hero of the war that would cost the French a great empire in America. It would launch George Washington, whose skirmish two years later with twenty Frenchmen is erroneously called the opening of the war, on a career of greatness.

When Awtawawtaw refused to return to Indiana, the Pennsylvania traders remained. Louis XV would not tolerate the loss of his rich trade and sent orders to the Marquis de Vaudrueil-Cavagnal, governor of French Canada, to bring the Indians back and drive out the traders by force. These orders were forwarded to Celeron, commander in the West at Michilmackinao (Mackinaw, Michigan). Celeron delegated the task, after two expeditions failed, to one of the most remarkable men who ever trod American soil—Charles Langlade.

Langlade was a hero and usually the leader in ninety-nine battles, and a leader of Indians without peer. Among his exploits was the crushing defeat of British General Edward Braddock near Fort Duquesne (now Pittsburgh, Pennsylvania) on July 9, 1755, the greatest defeat white men ever received from Indians. Langlade led a few half-breed relatives and 250 Ottawa and Chippewa warriors through several hundred miles of trackless wilderness. One morning, on June 21, 1752, they rushed out of the surrounding forest and assaulted the fort at Pickawillany. Most of the Miami braves were out hunting. As it was off season, only eight British traders were present. The invaders quickly killed more than a dozen Indians, one of the traders, and captured the rest, burning the fort.

Awtawawtaw, as a horrible example to any other chief who would trade with the British, was cut into small pieces, put into a big iron kettle, and made into soup which his savage foes ate. The Miamis learned their lesson so well that three years later two hundred and fifty of them, along with French settlers from Vincennes and Kekionga, helped their old enemy Langlade thrash the British and Americans, under Braddock.

The Treaty of Paris in 1763 put an end to most of the tomahawking and scalping of the pioneers and combatants. But Pontiac, chieftain of the Ottawas, had no love for the new British leaders nor for the Long-Knife frontiersman. He and eighteen tribes of Indians had not signed the treaty. They kept the war going for another two years, and with his Indians alone captured most of the tiny British forts all the way to Pittsburgh.

Because the local Miamis and the French traders connived with Pontiac, the two little forts at Kekionga and Ouiatenon in Indiana fell into Indian hands. Yet the Indians would not prevail for long. Detroit withstood a bitter siege, and the British soon recovered all their forts.

The lands along the Wabash and Ohio settled down to a decade of relative tranquility. Life went on much as before in the relentless quest for beaver by the same French and Indian inhabitants, except that it was directed by a handful of British traders out of Detroit. The British even abandoned the forts on the Wabash and Maumee, while new war clouds were gathering.

Col. Henry Bouquet, on orders of the British government, mobilized an army of 1,200 soldiers and frontiersmen at Fort Pitt, one of the largest armies ever in colonial times, and marched into Ohio to the Muskingum River against the Shawnees and other eastern tribes. Intimidated by such a show of force, they sued for peace, which was granted under the condition that they deliver up their captives. Two hundred and six whites were released at Pittsburgh.

But the Indians in present-day Indiana and to the west had not been subdued yet. When George Croghan, one of the Pennsylvania traders involved with the Indians at Pickawillany, was sent to negotiate with the Indians in the West, he was attacked by Kickapoos and Mascoutins on the Ohio, wounded, and his party nearly wiped out. Croghan was taken to Vincennes as a captive, where local Indians gained his release.

Despite the brilliant campaign of George Rogers Clark from 1779 to 1782 which established a toehold in the Old Northwest, Indiana was ruled by the Miamis and other allied Algonquin-speaking tribes for thirty years, from 1763 to 1795.

The Treaty of Paris of 1763 delivered all French possessions on the American continent to the English. King George III recognized the rights of the Indians to their land, which had never been relinquished by the tribes except for tiny grants of land, on loan, given the French for supporting their fur-trading posts. He issued a proclamation affirming that the land between the Alleghenies and the Mississippi be "reserved for the Indians." Strict penalties were enacted for any colonist who crossed the mountains and settled on the land.

The fur trade, which the French Crown had tried to control through the headquarters at Montreal, Mackinac, and Detroit, turned more or less into a shambles. The original French traders, and the English and Spanish traders from beyond the Mississippi, all indulged in a free-for-all, with little control. The British forts at Kekionga and Ouiatenon, taken by Pontiac, were not reoccupied by the British.

Avarice of the American colonists for the rich lands of the Ohio valley, and the equal determination of the Indians not to give them up, was a prime cause for the Revolutionary War that followed. Despite the Proclamation Line, rich and influential Americans including such prominent men as Benjamin Franklin and his son William as well as George Washington and his brother Lawrence speculated on the tremendous profits they could make by buying large tracts of western land and parceling them out to settlers. They acquired colonial grants to large areas, most of them illegal.

Otherwise, little of historic interest occurred during that period. An uneasy truce prevailed, and the haphazard fur trade continued. But settlers were drifting over the mountains, and speculators were wangling grants of land for which the Indians had not relinquished title. Serious friction with the Indians increased, and King George and Parliament responded with the Quebec Act in 1774 which enacted stricter penalties. It reaffirmed the Indians' rights, and placed all British land between the Alleghenies and the Mississippi under the control of the Canadian government at Quebec.

The Quebec Act served only to irritate the colonials, and helped to provoke the Revolution. The British never had a chance of enforcing the act to prevent the growing conflict with the Indians. Pioneers who had ventured over the mountains had already angered the Indians. Lord Dunsmore's War occurred the same year, in which for the first time a large group of backwoodsmen fought successfully against an equally large body of Indians.

The Battle of Point Pleasant on the Kanawha River was practically a draw, but it encouraged the backwoodsmen to believe they could settle the country.

west of the mountains despite Indian resistance. The settlers, however, who began trickling into Kentucky, Tennessee, and West Virginia (later Ohio), did not realize how united and stubborn that resistance would become.

Indiana entered this conflict in 1778 when a young Kentuckian, George Rogers Clark (who was a native of Virginia), talked Patrick Henry into sponsoring his tiny expedition to capture and hold certain territory which Virginia claimed under its colonial grants. This included most of the territory north of the Ohio. The expedition was secret, and neither the Virginia General Assembly nor Clark's men knew where they were headed.

The expedition was a brilliant success in its early stages. Kaskaskia and other settlements in southern Illinois were completely surprised and taken without battle. Vincennes was taken in another bloodless strike with the help of the French inhabitants who were not overly fond of the British but were overjoyed to learn that their mother country was now allied with the colonists. The French militia, on whom the British relied, simply agreed to serve the American flag instead of the British, as suggested by their priest, a Father Gibault.

Gov. Henry Hamilton, in turn, surprised Clark by boating 36 British regulars with a number of Indians and French settlers from Detroit down the Maumee and Wabash rivers. The French of Vincennes, not wanting to fight their Detroit relatives, deserted Capt. Leonard Helm and the two Americans holding Fort Sackville, who, of course, had to surrender.

Francis Vigo, an Italian trader from Spanish Louisiana, brought word of the capture to Clark. A daring exploit followed that has been the subject of many books. Clark set out in mid-February 1779 with 170 backwoodsmen

GEORGE ROGERS CLARK brought the American Revolution to Indiana soil when he occupied Fort Sackville, at Vincennes in July 1778. A local priest, Father Gibault, arranged the bloodless coup when the French militia, holding the fort for the British, turned it over to Clark.

CAPT. LEONARD HELM, a Pennsylvania Dutchman, was typical of Clark's frontier troops. He captured and was in charge of the fort at Vincennes. With only two men, he defied Gen. Henry Hamilton and 600 troops, including Indians, a few minutes before surrendering to the British in December 1779.

and French militia to retake Vincennes. They crossed Illinois and waded up to their armpits through icy flood waters, and then crossed the Wabash in boats.

Hamilton was completely surprised. It was his turn now to be deserted by his French allies during the siege of the fort, and he had only his 36 British regulars willing to fight.

As the French had stolen most of the powder from his magazine, Hamilton had to surrender after a short, almost bloodless siege, on February 25.

From then on, the Revolution in the Old Northwest became mostly a war of attrition. Clark and the new British commander, Capt. Richard B. Lernoult, both considered ambitious plans to attack each other during the next three years, but neither had enough men to dare the risk. Clark seldom had more than one hundred Americans plus the unreliable French militia; Captain Lernoult had only eighty British regulars.

Clark met all kinds of obstacles. Virginia, fighting three separate wars, was bankrupt, and yet he had to maintain and pay an army. According to historian Justin Winsor, Oliver Pollock, a rich American merchant living in Spanish-owned New Orleans, provided half of all monies required to support Clark's army. The reward of this true patriot, like that of Robert Morris of Philadelphia, was to be thrown in debtors' prison at the end of the war.

While Clark awaited his chance to attack Detroit, the British employed Indians to conduct bloody raids against the Kentucky settlements, mostly via routes east of Clark's forts. It has been estimated that fifteen hundred Kentuckians were killed in these raids, led by British officers, American Tories, or French militiamen. General Clark planned his last effort against Detroit in the summer of 1781, after recruiting more men in Pittsburgh.

SIMON KENTON, a giant Kentucky backwoodsman, was another of Clark's men. Historian Henry Howe, who knew the frontier intimately, stated that frontiersmen probably encountered more perils than any other men of the time. Kenton was a militia general under General Harrison in the War of 1812, and a scout with Anthony Wayne. Here, an early artist depicts Kenton rescuing the famous Daniel Boone from the Indians.

Disaster struck when British Indians, led by the educated Mohawk chief Joseph Brant, waylaid Col. Archibald Lochry and 130 Pennsylvania volunteer reinforcements at what is now Laughrey's Creek in Dearborn County.

Lochry's men were all killed or captured. Clark's last hope of taking Detroit vanished. From then on, the discouraged commander devoted his efforts to holding the forts he had captured, and to protecting Kentuckians from the British-led Indian raids. Clark's daring feats and the aid of Col. Rene Godefroy de Linctot, a most able French trader who was Virginia's agent to recruit Indians on the side of the Americans, had kept the western Indians loyal, or at least neutral.

Linctot died, probably of overwork, shortly afterward. Virtually all the tribes north of the Ohio joined the British-led raids against the hated "Long Knives," who were taking over land in Kentucky the Indians regarded as theirs.

The surrender of Cornwallis at Yorktown on October 19, 1781, ended the Revolution in the East. But not west of the mountains—that would last twelve more years. Kentucky would remain the "dark and bloody ground" for a long time to come. During the Revolution in the West, an obscure Indian had emerged briefly from the wilderness of the forks of the Wabash as the key figure in a mysterious expedition to take Detroit. Count Augustin de la Balme, a French officer who had come to America with Lafayette, organized a group of eighty Frenchmen at Vincennes and the Illinois towns. Without consulting Clark, he marched up the Wabash to Kekionga and took the tiny fort and trading post, occupied only by a few French traders and Indians.

But de la Balme's force made the mistake of plundering the trading post of Charles Beaubien, "the King's Man," representing British interests there. Beaubien had a Miami wife, Tacumwah, a most unusual Indian who had been married to another French fur trader. Her virtually unknown brother was Little Turtle, whose only claim to fame was the fact that he had gone on a few raids against the settlers in war parties led by his brother-in-law.

Beaubien sent a message to Little Turtle at his village on nearby Eel River. Little Turtle's Indians attacked the camp of the French on Aboite Creek and wiped out the la Balme expedition, killing many and capturing the rest, who were sent to Detroit in the summer of 1780.

The Miamis had been generally friendly to the Americans and remained so despite the la Balme affair until 1787, when the Northwest Ordinances were passed by Congress, and the Northwest Territorial Government organized. President Washington decided that Kekionga, the capital of the Miamis and other fugitive tribes, must be taken to make the territory safe for settlement.

On September 26, 1790, the U. S. Army, along with Kentucky and Pennsylvania militia, started from Cincinnati under Washington's instructions. Gen. Josiah Harmar was named commander-in-chief. It was the first U. S. Army campaign after the end of the Revolution. The army of 1,453 men found the teepees abandoned, burned the flimsy structures without opposition, and destroyed the Indians' food supplies. But Little Turtle had his Miamis lurking nearby who made two surprise attacks on Harmar's force, inflicting heavy losses, and sending Harmar into retreat.

Washington, who himself had considerable experience fighting Indians, made new plans. Gen. Arthur St. Clair, then stationed at Cincinnati, headquarters for the territory, was placed in overall command. There were a few attacks on villages on the Wabash which accomplished little more than the burning of more teepees and further infuriating the Indians. St. Clair, in the meantime, was organizing and training his army for the main expedition against Kekionga.

[27]

CHIEF LITTLE TURTLE of the Miamis has been acclaimed by many historians as the greatest American Indian who ever lived. Note his bear-claw necklace and the absence of an eagle-plume war bonnet. (FWPL)

CAPT. WILLIAM WELLS, captured as a boy, was the son-in-law and aide of Little Turtle. A resident of Fort Wayne, he died as the hero of the tragic Fort Dearborn massacre at Chicago in the War of 1812. (FWPL)

HYACINTH LASSELLE was the first white child born at present Fort Wayne, on February 25, 1777. His father was "the King's Man," the British agent in charge of recruiting Indians to fight the Americans. He later served as an American militia general in 1812, and wrote on the early history of the state. (FWPL)

JEAN BAPTISTE DE RICHARDVILLE, whose mother was sister to Little Turtle and whose father, a French fur trader, succeeded Little Turtle as chief of the Miamis. Fur trading at Fort Wayne for himself, he may have been a millionaire, and was called "America's Richest Indian." (FWPL)

FORT WAYNE as it appeared in 1794: Built by Gen. Anthony Wayne, it was preceded by three French and British forts on the same site. (FWPL)

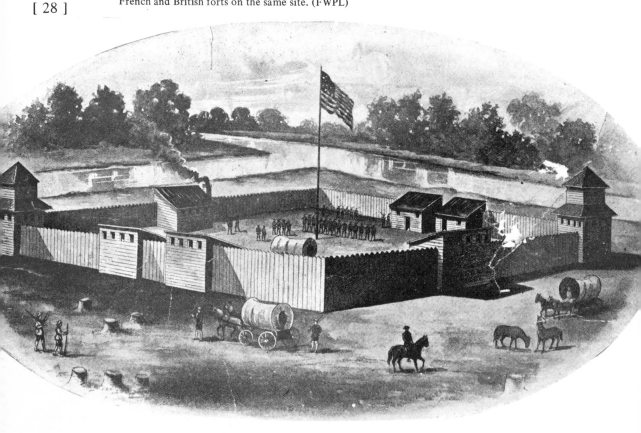

GEN. JOSEPH HARMAR, commander-in-chief of the U. S. Army, and his troops received a thorough whipping in October 1790 when they tried to take the Indian capital, Kekionga (Fort Wayne) from Little Turtle and the Miamis. This dignified portrait was undoubtedly painted in a happier moment. (FWPL)

St. Clair's army set out on September 17, 1791, following Harmar's old route through the wilderness, building forts to guard supplies on the way. The Miamis, headed by Little Turtle, had in the meantime gathered warriors from the Shawnees, Wyandots, Delawares, and other nearby tribes, creating a united force determined to stop the invaders.

These Indians had had a great deal of contact with the British, with Tories, and with the French, and their leader thought much like a white man. He organized his Indians by "messes" of ten warriors, explained their duties to them, and trained them for the battle ahead.

[29]

On November 3, St. Clair's army went into camp in a snowy opening near present-day Greeneville, Ohio, not far from its objective. The next morning,

GEN. ANTHONY WAYNE, "Mad Anthony," was the only leader President Washington found who could cope with the military genius of Little Turtle. The chief called him the "General Who Never Sleeps." This reputation came from the fact that the aged general was observed stomping around his camp at all times of night to be sure his sentries were awake.

COL. JOHN GIBSON, in spite of his civilized looks, was one of the greatest frontiersmen. As territorial secretary, he started Indiana's territorial government at Vincennes in the year 1800, while awaiting the arrival of Gov. William Henry Harrison. (ISL)

WILLIAM HENRY HARRISON, Indiana's first territorial governor, was the hero of Tippecanoe and the War of 1812. He became president in 1841 and, catching cold while delivering his inaugural address in the rain, died of pneumonia shortly afterward. Thus he was the first U.S. president to die in office. (VU)

GROUSELAND, Gov. Harrison's mansion at Vincennes, reflected the elegance of his native Virginia. It was built shortly after he became territorial governor in 1801, and is open to visitors today. (VU)

the troops were at breakfast when Little Turtle, who had planted his warriors in the woods surrounding the camp, attacked. General St. Clair went into battle with 1486 men. More than 1100 of them were killed or wounded by a force of fewer than 1000 Indians, whose attack was so skillfully managed that only 66 warriors were killed. St. Clair and the militia were blamed, and many alibis are given the whites in some accounts of the battle. The assessment by Col. Frederick Shaw, later commander of the Second Regiment which fought bravely in that battle, seems, however, to tell the whole story: "Their (the Indians') victory was clearly the result . . . of superior generalship."

Luckily for the Indians, Washington finally found Little Turtle's equal in Brig. Gen. Anthony Wayne, known as "Mad Anthony" because of his reckless courage. Little Turtle, observing that the "Blacksnake general never slept," respected his capability. Wayne had started toward the Miami capital in 1794, and Little Turtle suggested a night attack on his army near Greeneville. Overruled in council by other chiefs, he then counseled them to make peace, because the superior number and arms of the white man would eventually prevail.

The Indian council called Little Turtle a coward, deposed him as the war chief, and replaced him with a belligerent Shawnee, Blue Jacket. The two armies met on the banks of the Maumee at Fallen Timbers on August 20, 1794, and proved Little Turtle right. Wayne's army won a decisive victory in a short battle, with a loss of only 33 killed and 100 wounded.

The Treaty of Greeneville the next year finally ended the Revolution west of the mountains, and Indiana could be settled along with its neighboring states. On July 4, 1800, Indiana became a territory with Vincennes as its capital. Present-day Illinois, Michigan, and Wisconsin were included in its domain.

On July 22, John Gibson, a most remarkable man who had been appointed territorial secretary, arrived in Vincennes and organized the government of Indiana. As an Indian fighter and frontiersman, he was the equal of the Kentuckians—but the bald-headed Pennsylvanian fur trader had a far better education than most of the border heroes. He appointed both state and county officers, and organized the territorial militia. When Gov. William Henry Harrison, a Virginian, arrived six months later, a working government was ready for him.

Both Harrison and Gibson had fought in the armies sent against the Indians and had just the right experience to understand a frontier society. Harrison appointed three judges, and together the four men were empowered by President Jefferson to make whatever laws seemed appropriate, as long as they did not violate the Constitution of the United States.

With Indian opposition removed, little settlements began to spring up on the banks of the Ohio, at Madison, Aurora, Jeffersonville, Troy, New Albany, and Vevay. The Territorial Legislature organized and met for the first time in 1805. The hard work of settling and clearing the land along the rivers went on. Flatboats brought more immigrants to the fertile Hoosier land. The Army maintained garrisons at two forts, one at Fort Knox (Terre Haute) and the other at Fort Wayne. There was virtually no trouble with the Indians, and government was efficient.

By 1810, population was still small in the territory but had passed 24,000. A small number of industrial enterprises sprang up to augment the two main activities, farming and fur trade. The industries were primitive pork packing establishments, saw- and gristmills, maple sugar production, and cottage industries.

But clouds of trouble were rising on the horizon. Tecumseh, a Shawnee Indian, was deluded by a vision that the Indians, if they would only unite, would get substantial help from the British across the border and could throw the "Long Knives" out of the Old Northwest. No major chief of the northwestern tribes aided him, but with the able help of his brother, The Prophet, who was a medicineman, and the encouragement of the British in Canada, he gathered seven hundred rebellious warriors on the Wabash at the mouth of the Tippecanoe. On November 7, 1811, while Tecumseh was away, the Indians attacked an army of 910 white men, mostly U. S. regulars and Indiana militia, commanded by General Harrison, who had marched to the village to intimidate it into breaking up.

White losses were heavy with 62 dead and 126 wounded, but the Indians were repelled and fled Tippecanoe. Yet the white victory, nevertheless, only antagonized the Indians even more and failed to halt the growing revolt.

The War of 1812 began in June that year. Tecumseh's horde of Indians was easily repelled by tiny, greatly outnumbered garrisons at Fort Harrison and Fort Wayne. Twenty-four settlers, mostly women and children, were brutally massacred by the Indians at Pigeon Roost in Scott County. Earlier, in August, the war in the West had opened with the Fort Dearborn massacre that occurred in the sand dunes along Lake Michigan, just west of the Indiana

AARON BURR, one of the most controversial and romantic characters in U.S. history, fled to Jeffersonville, Indiana, after the famous duel on July 11, 1804, in which he killed Alexander Hamilton. At the Indiana town, he hatched plans and recruited men for his mysterious armed expedition down the Mississippi River, which resulted in his trial for treason. Among his prominent recruits at Jeffersonville were Maj. Davis Floyd and Alexander Ralston, who later surveyed the site for Indianapolis when it was laid out as the capital.

THE FIRST METHODIST EPISCOPAL CHURCH in the state was this log structure at Charlestown. Built in 1807, it was purchased and restored by the Indiana conference in 1902. (ISL)

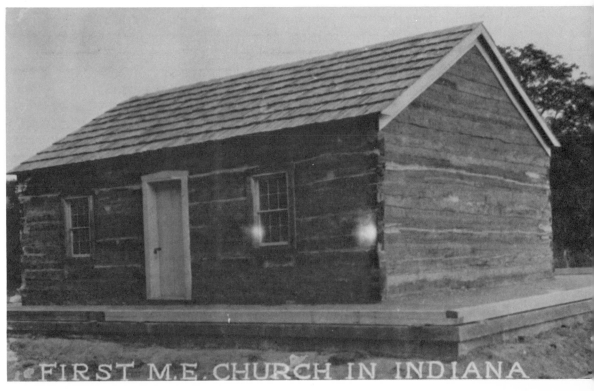

FIRST M.E. CHURCH IN INDIANA

THE BATTLE OF TIPPECANOE, fought on November 7, 1811, is commemorated by this fine monument, erected by Sen. John Tipton, who purchased the site and gave it to the state. The rectangular marker shows the spot where "The Prophet," leader of the Indian village, implored the Great Manitou during the battle to charm the white man's bullets against striking the Indians, as he had promised them. The charm failed to work.

THE BATTLE OF THE MISSISSINEWA, fought on December 18, 1812, between 600 white soldiers led by Col. John Campbell and the Miami Indians near LaFontaine, is commemorated by this humble marker. The white victory kept the Miamis from taking further part in the War of 1812. As important as Tippecanoe, the site would have remained unmarked, had not Cora Straughan, a Marion High School history teacher, marshalled her class in 1922 to gather fieldstones and cement them together.

border. Capt. William Wells, the white Miami son-in-law of Little Turtle, who had led a party of Miamis to help the American garrison, was killed.

Most of the Miamis and Delawares, faithful to the treaty they had signed at Greeneville, tried to remain neutral. The Miamis left Kekionga and other villages to join their fellow tribesmen in the more remote Mississinewa River area. Harrison, who by now had been placed at the head of the western army, set out to regain Detroit from the British.

Some of the Miamis had massacred a few settlers, and a few had taken part in the siege of Fort Wayne, though most favored peace. Fearing a potentially hostile army in his rear, Harrison sent Col. John B. Campbell with six hundred U. S. Regulars and Pennsylvania and Ohio militiamen to destroy the Mississinewa towns. After destroying three villages, this force was attacked on December 17, 1812, by three hundred Miamis and Munsees, and

MAJ. HUGH McGARY, a Kentucky frontiersman, founded and ran a ferry at Evansville in 1812. An impetuous militia leader, he was blamed for the disastrous defeat of Kentuckians at the battle of Blue Licks on the Licking River in Kentucky. Daniel Boone, another leader, had warned that Simon Girty and his Indians might be planning an ambush—and they had.

[35]

FLATBOATS carried immigrants, their household "plunder," and their produce to market for several decades as Indiana was being settled. First used on the Ohio River, every Indiana river and creek that could float the shallow-draft boats in floodtime had such craft until the steamboats and railroads took their place.

THE SHAKERS, a religious group which prohibited marriage and practiced communal living, built a thriving settlement at West Union (Shakertown) north of Vincennes. With the War of 1812, they fled to Kentucky, but later returned. They were heckled by Methodist circuit riders and others, which led the community to move back east after the Civil War. (Harper's)

repelled them in a sharp battle. Fearing Indian reinforcements, the little army retreated to Ohio, since most of its horses had been killed, and supplies were low. This battle did, however, discourage most Miamis and Delawares from taking part in the war. The Pottawattomies and other Indiana tribes joined the British army in Canada under the leadership of Tecumseh.

General Harrison's army and Oliver Hazard Perry's little navy on Lake Erie provided one of the bright spots in the dismal record of Americans in the War of 1812. It had been a disaster in the East. The nation might have been reconquered if Britain had not at the same time been busy fighting Napoleon, an antagonist difficult enough for any nation.

Thus, the Americans were able to retake Detroit, and General Harrison chased the British army under Gen. Henry A. Proctor across the Detroit River where he cornered it and its Indian allies at the Thames River. The ensuing battle was a rout, Tecumseh was killed, and Proctor fled. General Harrison became a hero and was considered presidential timber.

John Gibson had taken over the governorship and home defense during the war. The capital had been moved to Corydon. With peace, settlers arrived in large numbers. By 1816, Indiana was ready for statehood, with Jon-

GEN: WILLIAM HENRY HARRISON watches his troops crossing Lake Erie before the crucial battle of the Thames near Detroit against the British and Indians on October 5, 1812. The British were crushed in the West, and Tecumseh became a dead hero.

ZACHARY TAYLOR, who later became the 12th president, is shown in his first military engagement, in which he and about a dozen soldiers held off Tecumseh and 200 Indians who attacked and burned part of Fort Harrison (now Terre Haute) on September 4-5, 1812. The men held off the Indians, and built a barricade at the corner of the log fort where a blockhouse had burned away.

THE *NEW ORLEANS*, shown as a replica built in its centennial year, 1911, made one of the most dramatic and historic voyages in history in November 1811, when it chugged down the Ohio and Mississippi Rivers, opening the great steamboat traffic to New Orleans. The New Madrid earthquake, occurring at the time, made the trip terrifying. (ISL)

ANNA HARRISON, wife of one president, William Henry Harrison, and grandmother of another, Benjamin Harrison, never set foot in the White House. She lived in Vincennes in Indiana territorial days, and retired with her husband after statehood to North Bend, Ohio, just across the state line.

ALEX COQUILLARD, a French fur trader from Detroit, arrived in Indiana in 1820, and soon became one of northern Indiana's leading movers and shakers. He is called the founder of South Bend, originally dubbing it St. Joseph Station.

THE FIRST STATE CAPITOL of Indiana was this charming little two-room building at Corydon, built of limestone from a neighboring quarry. Prior to 1816 it had served a short while as Territorial Capital, and before that, as the Harrison County Courthouse. Well-preserved by the state, it appears much as it did originally.

INDIANAPOLIS WAS CHOSEN as the new state capital by a commission headed by Christopher Harrison of Salem. This painting shows the surveyors who laid out the embryo city, as they camped on the site in 1823. The stream probably is Pogue's Run, and the Indians probably are of the Delaware tribe, who lived on White River. (ISL)

MARION COUNTY COURTHOUSE at Indianapolis, built in 1823-4: It served as a temporary State Capitol after completion. State Treasurer Samuel Merrill moved the State Treasury there from Corydon in two wagons. (ISL)

THE MADISON AND INDIANAPOLIS RAILROAD was Indiana's first. This print represents the train, but can give no suggestion of how miserable the track was. (ISL)

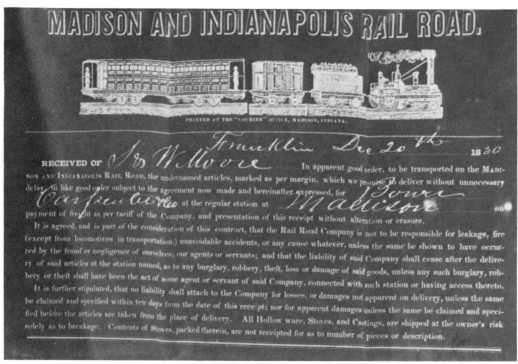

athan Jennings from New Jersey as its first state governor. The treaty of St. Mary's with the Indians opened most of central Indiana for settlement.

By 1820, population had reached 147,178. Among its new settlers were Thomas Lincoln and family, who came to Spencer County from Kentucky. Peace and tranquility brought fast development during the next decade, and Indiana's major transportation routes were a big factor. Steamboats thronged the Ohio, Wabash, and even smaller rivers, and construction of the National and Michigan roads was begun. Immigrants streamed to the north end of the state in increasing numbers in the 1830s. Education became of importance, and various colleges were founded. Indiana had made the transition from a wilderness frontier to a pioneer society.

WILLIAM CONNER, a fur trader born in an Indian village, was one of Indiana's fascinating and important men. He settled his trading post north of present Indianapolis in 1800, when central Indiana had no other inhabitants but Indians. In 1823, he built this elegant mansion while the area was still wilderness. Purchased and restored by Eli Lilly, Jr., the mansion is today a public museum at Conner Prairie Farm, near Noblesville. (ISL)

LORENZO DOW, probably best-known of all the pioneer circuit riders, was a modern Elijah. When he visited Indiana, he would dash on a horse from the woods into a backwoods community, dismount, and preach with such fire and fervor he became known as "Crazy" Dow.

ALLEN HAMILTON was an attorney at Fort Wayne who, like many leading men of early Indiana, became rich in the fur trade. He arrived at Fort Wayne in 1823 and served as adviser to chiefs Richardville and Meshingomesia. (FWPL)

ROBERT OWEN OF SCOTLAND *(below right)* was a wealthy reformer and industrialist who bought the Rappite Village of Harmonie and, renaming it New Harmony, began in 1825 an experiment based on community ownership and equality of work and profit. Scientists and scholars flocked to the new Utopia, but the experiment failed in 1827. The town remained, nevertheless, as an educational, cultural, and scientific center until the Civil War. "Women's lib" had an advocate then, too, in Frances Wright *(below left)*, an eloquent and beautiful Englishwoman who started an ultra-liberal magazine, *The New Harmony Gazette*, together with Robert Dale Owen, son of the founder. When the experiment collapsed, Wright and Owen moved to New York where they edited the *Free Enquirer*, and attempted to start a Workingmen's Party. (Lockwood)

MARTIN BOOTS, first permanent white settler of Marion, built this log cabin here in 1826. It is now the star attraction of the museum in Matter Park.

THE OLD NATIONAL ROAD *(below)* the first U.S. Highway, was only a rutty, cleared path through the woods when it first reached Indiana in 1829. It was extended to Terre Haute in 1835, running down Washington Street in Indianapolis. Extended to St. Louis, it was the greatest eastern immigrant route, and later became US-40. Many immigrants to the West *(above)* got their first view of the great American prairies in western Indiana. (ISL)

JOHNNY APPLESEED, legendary hero and patron saint of the pioneers, was John Chapman in real life. He shrewdly planted his apple seeds in little nurseries in the wilderness in the early 1800s, so the trees would be of bearing age a decade later when the immigrants arrived. This sketch by a Miami University student who knew him is considered a good likeness of the eccentric wanderer, who died in 1847 and is buried in Fort Wayne, where his grave can still be seen.

THE BATTLE OF BAD-AXE in Illinois, in which many Hoosier militiamen took part, ended Black Hawk's War in 1832 and one of the worst panics Indiana ever knew. The old chief had brought his tribesmen from west of the Mississippi to plant corn and pumpkins at the former Sauk and Fox village site, which had earlier been given up by a treaty. The Indiana grapevine bristled with rumors during the time, especially since Black Hawk and his warriors had dashed through the northwest part of the state, via the Old Sauk Trail, on their way to see friends in British Canada. Blockhouses were built in many towns and militia companies were mustered for the state's defense, although the war never touched Indiana.

Indiana from 1830 to 1860

ALTHOUGH INDIANA never had serious threats from the Indians after the War of 1812, it had considerable excitement at times. In 1831, Chief Black Hawk came home from a winter hunt with his band on the prairies west of the Mississippi to find white squatters had taken over the land near the point where the Rock River enters the Great River in Illinois. His Sauks had occupied the site for half a century.

He took his warriors by way of the Great Sauk Trail across Northwest Indiana, which was very sparsely settled indeed, to Malden, across the St. Clair River in Canada. There, the British commander advised him to stand up for "his rights." The farce known as Black Hawk's War ensued. Nearly all of northern Indiana was still frontier. Rumors ran rampant that several little settlements in the northwest part of the state had been wiped out. Actually, the Sauks never came near the borders during the war.

Blockhouse forts were built at LaPorte and several other settlements. U.S. Senator John Tipton, a former Indian fighter and hero of Tippecanoe, quickly got a bill through Congress to raise 600 Indiana Rangers to join General Scott's regular Army which was pursuing Chief Black Hawk. The militia was mustered in Indianapolis and in most settlements of any size. It marched and countermarched, protecting the state's citizens and chasing down rumors. Black Hawk's band was routed at Bad Axe on August 2, 1832.

This uprising led to demands for the removal of Indians who still occupied Indiana land. Treaties were soon concluded with both the Pottawattomies and the Miamis which allowed removal of most of them to reservations in Kansas. In the final treaty confirmed in 1840, a ten-square-mile reservation on the Mississinewa River was set aside for the Meshingomesia band of the Miami Indians.

Indiana entered a new era in 1830. In the next two decades transportation routes were developed pell-mell. Industry began to develop as a viable factor of life. Most of the Indians—those stumbling blocks to the path of the plow—had been removed, and emigrants streamed north to occupy their former homes. The state was gripped in the great anti-slavery movement. Primitive transportation gave way to steamboats, railroads, and canals. The pageant of Indiana's growth was an exciting, fast-changing scenario. By 1850, only 34 years after becoming a state, Indiana became one of the great states, and a leader in the nation.

The slavery question had become a vital national issue. Although many citizens of southern descent dissented, Indiana stood politically with the New England states, opposed to slavery. Although their numbers were relatively small, the Friends, or Quakers, vociferously agitated against slavery verbally and in abolition newspapers.

They provided the backbone of the organization of the Underground Railroad, which began to function in Indiana in 1831. The Fugitive Slave Law permitted southern slave owners to pursue their fleeing "chattels" north of the Mason and Dixon Line. Indiana citizens were required by law, whenever called on, to assist the slave owners, but the plight of the wretched fugitives usually produced the opposite effect. Many other churches joined the Quakers in this informal underground organization.

Zealous men were posted with skiffs all along the Ohio River to watch for and to assist fleeing blacks. They were spirited to some friendly farmhouse by night and were aided in reaching Michigan on the way to Canada, with sympathizers hiding them at convenient stops. Madison, New Albany, Rockport, Evansville, Jeffersonville, and Cincinnati all were well-known crossing places into Indiana. There were three especially prominent routes. In the west, the slaves were smuggled northward through Princeton and Petersburg; from the Louisville area through Salem, Bloomington, and Indianapolis to the Quaker settlements to the north of the Capital; in the east, the busiest route

[46]

TOM AND ABE LINCOLN built this cabin in 1830 in Macon County, Illinois, upon their arrival from Indiana, shortly before Abe left home to make his own way. The photo was taken after the cabin had been abandoned. (ISL)

THE WABASH RIVER NEAR VINCENNES as it appeared in 1834: The artist was the famed Carl Bodmer, who accompanied Prince Maximilian von Neuwied and his scientists to study at New Harmony and elsewhere. (VU)

of all was the one converging on New Garden (later changed to Newport and Fountain City). Here was the home of Levi Coffin, prosperous merchant and prominent Quaker, who came to be known nationally as "conductor of the Underground Railroad." It is reported that he personally sheltered in his home more than two thousand runaways.

Spurred on by the actual contact with fleeing slaves, Indianans became intensely gripped by the bitter issue of slavery. Anti-slavery forces were marshaled together under the banner of the Republican party in the state which was organized in 1856. The refusal of Democratic Gov. Joseph A. Wright to to place the resources of the state behind the plea of abolitionists in the "Bloody Kansas" troubles intensified the feeling of the people, and increased political division. In the election of 1856, the newly-formed Republicans trailed by a narrow margin. They won by an equally narrow margin in 1860 over the pro-slavery Democrats.

Road building began in earnest in 1832 when, after the Pottawattomies had ceded a narrow strip of land for a road north of the Wabash River, work was begun on the "old Michigan road" which led from the Ohio River port of Madison (then the state's largest town) to a small fur-trading post known as South Bend. It was to connect the Ohio River with the Great Lakes at Michigan City. It was not much of a road, as most of the $150 per mile was spent to cut trees low enough for wagons to pass over the stumps. For four months of the year, the road was virtually as impassable as the Kankakee Swamps (which had been bypassed) because of the deep mud. During winter, or when it was dry in summer, the unsurfaced road fulfilled its purpose well.

Covered wagons streamed north, following the road contractors as they progressed and even forging ahead of them to become the first to claim the

LEOPOLD POKAGON, Chief of the Pottawattomis, (painted in 1838) who lived near South Bend, is remembered mainly for selling much of northern Indiana and Illinois, including the site of Chicago, for a few cents per acre to the United States in the treaty of 1833. He made a better deal than the Indians who traded Manhattan Island for beads. (NIHS)

[48]

GEORGE WINTER, famous pioneer painter of Logansport and Lafayette, painted these Indians from life while they were at camp along the upper Wabash River in the late 1830s.

rich land. By 1840, with the aid of the Wabash and Erie canal, pioneer settlements were spotted in clearings, usually on a stream where a grist and saw mill could be located, throughout the north half of the state.

Construction of the Wabash and Erie canal, which would become the longest in the world when completed in its 612-mile route from Lake Erie to Evansville, was started at Fort Wayne. Progress was slow as it went westward, and there were many problems. In a way, the canal era in Indiana was a fiasco as the canals cost ten times as much as estimated because of graft, corruption, and the ignoring of sound economics. Indiana, along with Michigan, would go bankrupt before it was finished. But the frenzy was exciting while it lasted, and the two canals finally constructed, out of the many planned, speeded settlement.

CROSSROADS OF THE UNITED STATES: The map shows the transportation routes by water, land, and rail which cross the continent through Indiana.

[49]

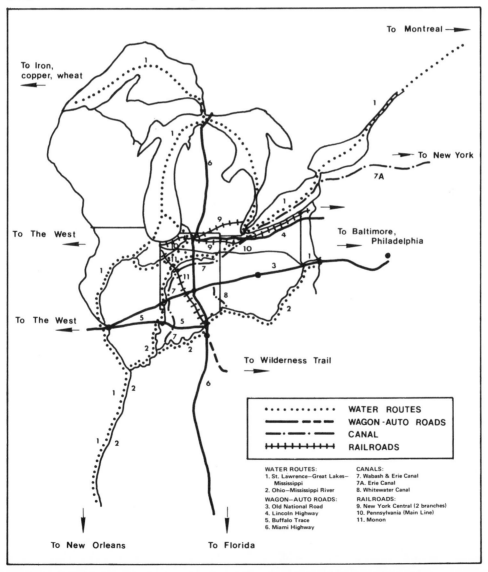

WATER ROUTES
WAGON-AUTO ROADS
CANAL
RAILROADS

WATER ROUTES:
1. St. Lawrence—Great Lakes—
   Mississippi
2. Ohio—Mississippi River
WAGON—AUTO ROADS:
3. Old National Road
4. Lincoln Highway
5. Buffalo Trace
6. Miami Highway

CANALS:
7. Wabash & Erie Canal
7A. Erie Canal
8. Whitewater Canal
RAILROADS:
9. New York Central (2 branches)
10. Pennsylvania (Main Line)
11. Monon

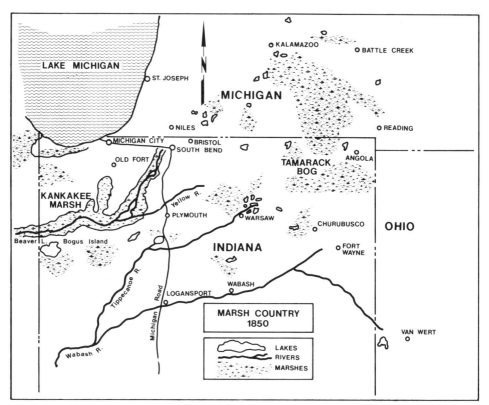

NORTHERN INDIANA HARBORED many horse thieves, counterfeiters, cutthroats, and general no-goods before its many marshes were drained and cleared for the plow. This map shows the locations of the principal marshes and the state's two largest lakes, Beaver and English, which disappeared when the Kankakee marshes were finally drained. Bogus Island in Beaver Lake was a famous desperado hideout.

OLD SILE DOTY, who stole horses in the United States, Canada, Mexico, and England, gloried in his prowess and told about it in his memoirs. His main haunts from 1834 to 1876 were on the northern Indiana border. He organized other rascals from the northern part of the state into a ring which made life miserable for horse owners.

[50]

MESHINGOMESIA was the last real tribal chief of the Miami Indians, presiding over the Metocinyah Reservation of ten square miles on the Mississinewa River in Wabash and Grant counties, from 1839 until his death in 1879. The reservation, the only Indiana land owned in common by the tribe after 1839, was broken up in 1880. From 150 to 1500 Indians, including two captive white girls and a few Delawares and Pottawattomis lived there during his time. (Goodpasture)

Meshingomesia
Chief.

WAUCACOONAH, called Waucoon by his white neighbors, was a young Pottawattomi convert of Father Pettit. He escaped when Gen. John Tipton and 100 soldiers surrounded the Indians' Catholic Church near Twin Lakes, Marshall County, and captured the congregation in September 1838. They deported the reluctant Indians to a reservation in Kansas, but Waucoon hid in a hollow tree, and then walked nearly one hundred miles through the woods to escape the infamous "Trail of Death." Chief Meshingomesia had the boy formally adopted into the Miami tribe, where he grew to become a Baptist preacher and farmer. Substituting for the regular ministers at the Baptist Church on the reservation, he also built a frame church for the Indians on his farm west of LaFontaine, which is still standing today. He died in 1882. (Goodpasture)

FRANCIS LA FONTAINE, son of a French trader and an Indian mother, was named chief of the Miamis who were taken to Kansas from 1841 to 1846, the years of the emigration. He was deposed by the Miamis when they found he would not stay in Kansas with them, and when he died in Lafayette on his return his family maintained he had been given a slow poison. (FWPL)

THE COTTON MILL at Cannelton, erected in 1840 of locally quarried sandstone, was probably the first substantial factory built in Indiana. Great sternwheelers brought cotton up the Mississippi and Ohio to unload at the Cannelton wharf boat *(below)*. The mill, although idle, still stands. (ISL)

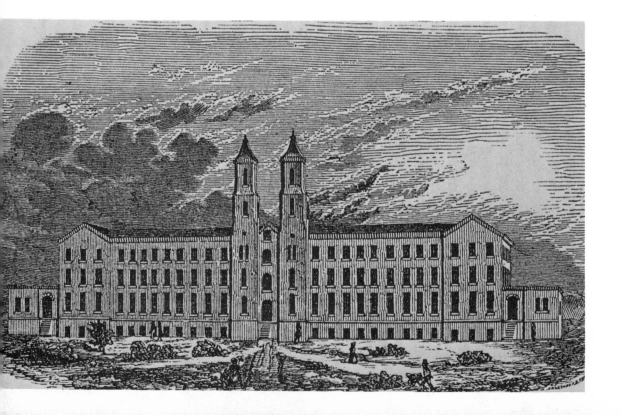

THE FIRST GOVERNOR'S RESIDENCE was built at Illinois and Market in Indianapolis, which later became the location of the world's largest traction-car terminal. Gov. David Wallace first occupied it in 1837. (ISL)

SMITH & HANNA'S GROCERY, erected in 1842, was the first building at the Odd Fellow Corner in Indianapolis. Note the pigs in the foreground, doing garbage detail, common in many cities at that time. Christian Schrader did this sketch from memory in 1907. (ISL)

USING A STUMP ROSTRUM, a political orator rated as a prime diversion in 1841, when there were no TV, X-rated movies, or baseball leagues. Orating here at Indianapolis on January 8 is Isaac Montgomery of Gibson County. (ISL)

[53]

"THE HOOSIER'S NEST" was the title given to this painting done about 1850 by Monimia Bunnell, devoted wife of Samuel S. Boyd, to depict John Finley's poem, in which the first printed use of the word "hoosier" occurs. The painting illustrated the subject so faithfully that the State Legislature asked that it be donated to the State Library, which was done. When an Indianapolis newspaper critic publicly decried her primitive technique, Monimia's physician husband stole it from the library and took it home to his heart-broken wife. (ISL)

[54]

NEWSPAPER EDITORS also printed and bound books, and tended the postoffice in the early days, as here in Indianapolis in 1850. (ISL)

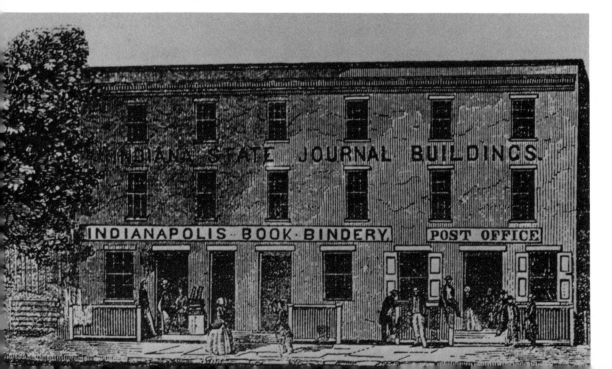

ELEGANT AND STYLISH SIDE-wheelers dominated Southern Indiana transportations prior to the Civil War. The twelve stars the artist put in the flag seem to indicate that the *Bradish Johnson* operated about 1776–but 1840 is more likely. (ISL)

DEAD MAN'S BOAT was what they called this type of horsedrawn barge which operated on the Wabash and Erie Canal in the 1840s and 1850s. It was so called since crew watchmen, on top the cabin, were sometimes swept off by overhanging bridges and tree limbs to drown in the dark. (FWHS)

JENNY LIND, the "Swedish Nightingale," arrived in New York in 1850, brought over by P. T. Barnum. It was the greatest cultural event in America up to that time. The smallest place she visited in her three-year triumphal tour was Madison, Indiana (pop. 6,000), where the pioneer women were determined to have culture–with or without opera house. They cleaned, scrubbed, and whitewashed the pork slaughterhouse, idle in summer, and decorated it with green boughs. Barnum, getting off the steamboat, said she would not sing in such a monstrosity. But Jenny Lind was a gallant trouper and sang anyway!

[55]

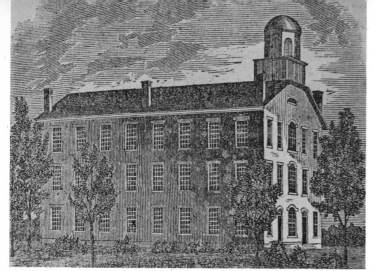

INDIANA UNIVERSITY'S
first building at Bloomington,
depicted in 1850, when enroll-
ment approached two hundred.

ST. MARY'S ACADEMY, later a college, as it appeared about 1854: The institution now is located
across US-31 from the Notre Dame University campus at South Bend—which was then at Bertrand,
Michigan. (NIHS)

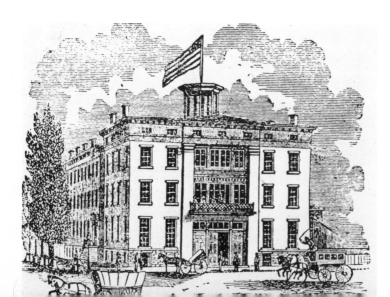

THE ROCKHILL HOUSE in
Fort Wayne at Main and Broad-
way was the city's earliest first-
class hotel. Construction began
in 1838, and it is shown at the
time of completion in 1854.
(FWPL)

"WRONG WAY CORRIGAN" of Indiana was the balloon *Jupiter*, surrounded here by an excited throng near the present courthouse site at Lafayette on August 16, 1859. With 123 letters in a mailbag, it was to carry the first U. S. airmail to New York. Conditions weren't right until the next day, and then the balloon took off heading south instead of east, and was forced to land at Crawfordsville, only twenty-seven miles away. Still, it was airmail, and it was official! (ISL)

HUGH B. MCCULLOUGH of Fort Wayne, cashier of the city's first bank, surely was one of America's greatest financial experts. He set up the first sound banking system in Indiana, and in 1859, as U. S. comptroller of the currency, the first federal banking system. As secretary of the treasury under Lincoln and Johnson, he became unpopular by predicting that the greenback currency inflation, if not halted, would bring the greatest panic the nation had ever known. Grant replaced him in the cabinet. But, Mc-Cullough's prediction came true in 1873, and President Charles Arthur reinstated him to the cabinet.

INDIANAPOLIS HAD VISIONS that the White River was navigable, and that, with a little dredging and straightening, it would make the capital a busy port. Among several steamers hoping to claim the reward for being first to reach the city is this unidentified craft that was wrecked at the railroad bridge in Waverly, sixteen miles away. (ISL)

[58]

THE PACKET *O. P. MORTON*, during high water in 1859, was the only steamer ever to reach Indianapolis. Behind the steamer loaded with dignitaries of the city is the covered bridge, a part of the Old National Road, built in 1836 at Washington Street. (ISL)

The Civil War Years: 1860 to 1865

THE ATTACK of Union Soldiers on Fort Sumter in April, 1861, brought an end to tranquility in Indiana—which had grown to become the sixth state of the nation in population. It now had well-organized routes of transportation. From a frontier area it had become a bustling, prosperous, important cog in the United States.

Although with the exception of Morgan's cavalry raid of 1863, the actual fighting was elsewhere, Hoosiers were at first in turmoil and divided in allegiance. A slim majority supported Indiana-reared President Lincoln in the election who stated in his inaugural address that it mattered not whether slavery remained or was abolished, as he was sworn by his oath to preserve the Union, and he would do so. Oliver Perry Morton, gubernatorial candidate of the new Republican Party, barely squeaked through himself.

The Douglas Democrats believed after the election that the South could be brought back into the Union by compromise and conciliation. Possibly, with their strong roots in Kentucky, Tennessee, Virginia, and other mid-Atlantic states, a majority of the native-born Hoosiers had close relatives fighting in the Rebel forces. A small minority even felt so deeply in sympathy with the slaveowners that they were involved in serious sabotage and sedition. Apparently, there was a very real clandestine conspiracy among southern sympathizers not only in Indiana but also in neighboring states to organize an armed uprising in the West to support the South. This was carried on through various secret organizations such as the Knights of the Golden Circle, the Peanutters, etc.

Some modern scholars have tried to dismiss this conspiracy as imaginary, or a straw enemy created by Governor Morton and other Union leaders. In

ABRAHAM LINCOLN passed through Indiana, the state where "he was raised," with much of the rough Hoosier homespun stamp still upon him. He was on his way to Washington and the presidency in the nation's most trying time. On his next visit he would be lying in state as the martyred victim of an assassin's bullet.

nearly every one of the ninety-two Indiana counties, however, Union recruiters have been bushwhacked and killed, and wholesale desertions of conscripted men occurred. Newspapers supporting or opposing the Union Cause were attacked by mobs, and their printing presses destroyed.

An indication of the extent of the movement and the strength of feeling was the "Battle of Pogue's Run." Governor Morton had received word that Democratic legislators and supporters coming to Indianapolis by train for a meeting were armed, and that a shoot-out might occur. The governor alerted the Union Army who stopped the train and searched it and its passengers. When the Democratic politicians saw the soldiers, they pitched their pistols out of the windows into a wooded ravine, and the "battle" was squelched before it started.

Morton was a strong man who, despite some opposition, kept Indiana loyal to Lincoln and the Union Army. At the beginning of the war, his call for troops was met quickly, and soldiers raised all over the state.

But as the war did not come to an end as speedily as expected and incompetent Union generals were defeated time and again by the brilliant tactics of Gen. Robert E. Lee and his fellow commanders, the opposition of certain Indiana leaders, though probably more political than treasonous, became more flagrant and inexcusable. The election of fall 1862 was won by a Democrat by a very narrow margin, rather than by a Republican—and all the while the Union armies faced some of their darkest hours.

The meeting of the General Assembly in early 1863 was in a shambles, even going so far as to fail to appropriate funds for recruiting and equipping troops. One Indiana historian, Logan Esarey, called it a "disgrace to both parties and the state," and "the most unworthy in the state's history."

Morton weathered the crisis by borrowing money on his own personal credit and that of James F. D. Lanier, a former Hoosier, who had become a railroad magnate in New York. As the Union armies gained the upper hand

and ultimate victory became inevitable, Hoosiers forgot their disputes and rallied behind Morton to make significant contributions to the Union cause. 76,242 men, mostly farm youths, served in the Union Army, and Indiana supplied two-and-a-half million horses and draft animals, more than any other state in the nation.

The state was one of the top two or three producers of wheat, corn, hogs, cattle, sheep, and potatoes. The great wealth of northern farms is said to have been a factor that turned the tide in the war, and Indiana contributed much more than its share in these vital foodstuffs. Its geography even assisted logistics—since most of its early railroads and canals led directly south toward the front.

Before the beginning of the nineteenth century, Hamburg, Germany, claimed to be the "pork packing center of the world," but was replaced by Cincinnati after the turn of the century. The Midwest corn-hog belt, developed by the pioneers who had arrived from the East, became one of the most efficient meat production systems devised.

But by the time of the Civil War, the packing business moved further west as pioneers in Indiana and Illinois cleared land and raised hogs and corn. Indianapolis took the title away from Cincinnati, to hold it until the late 1800s when Chicago became "hog butcher to the world." The capital city was so proud of the title that the commissioners of Marion County, where it is located, decreed that the county seal be a circle, enclosing a prime, fat porker, otherwise unadorned. In the 1960s, however, the commissioners in

[61]

BUSTLING INDIANAPOLIS was the crossroads of the nation as it mobilized the state's resources for the Union in the early part of the Civil War. This remarkable W. H. Bass photo of 1862 shows Washington Street, looking east from Meridian. (ISL)

GEN. AMBROSE BURNSIDE, sporting the splendid side-whiskers that made his name immortal, is shown directing the Union landing force at New Berne, North Carolina. Raised at Liberty, Union County, he was the most eminent of Indiana's generals, and succeeded McClellan as commander of the Army of the Potomac. His name is now a household word, since side-whiskers like his came to be known as burnsides, later changed to sideburns.

HOOSIER HYSTERIA meant something other than basketball in July 1863, when Gen. John Hunt Morgan, the noted Confederate cavalry leader, and "Morgan's Terrible Men" dashed across southeastern Indiana (from Mauckport to the Ohio line), with Union troops and farmers in hot pursuit. (Leslie's)

their infinite wisdom decided that the seal was unseemly, and substituted a far less significant design.

The Indiana meat packing industry, which was important at Madison and other cities as well, made a substantial contribution to the war effort. The Van Camp Company at Indianapolis, just starting in the then-infant canning business, ingeniously developed a Civil-War type of "C-rations" known as pork and beans.

The Studebaker brothers, wagonmakers at South Bend who had started in business in 1852 and built two wagons the next two years, became an industrial giant with Army contracts. One of the rare and unusual Currier and Ives lithographs shows a Civil War encampment scene, entitled simply "10,000 Studebaker Wagons."

Indiana contributed few generals with outstanding records. The highest-ranking was Maj. Gen. Ambrose Burnside, who replaced the dilatory McClellan in defeating General Morgan in Kentucky and in the East Tennessee campaign. A Rush County native, he was a West Point graduate and a veteran of the Mexican war.

One of the least-noted but possibly most significant happenings of the entire war took place outside the Union Railway Station at Indianapolis. The Union Army had suffered another great defeat at Chickamauga after a fairly auspicious start in an attempt at cutting the South in two. Union troops had pulled back to Chattanooga, and a pall of gloom fell over the North as it was learned that the Army of the Cumberland was under siege and in a critical position.

The situation seemed so perilous that President Lincoln was routed out of bed, and a war council held. Ulysses S. Grant, whose Vicksburg and Shiloh battles were among the few notable Union victories, received a telegram, ordering him to report to Louisville to confer with an official of the War Department. En route, his train stopped at Indianapolis. Just after the train left the station there, it was halted, and Secretary of War Edward Stanton appeared himself with a message to Grant from the commander-in-chief, President Lincoln.

Lincoln's patience had become exhausted with lethargic and bumbling generals. He had created a new Army of the Mississippi, and Grant was notified that he was its commander. Its brilliant success in dividing the South with Sherman's march to the sea spelled the doom of the Confederacy. Grant was named commander of all the armies, and the war was won which might well have dragged on for years had it not been for the dramatic appointment on Indiana soil.

Perhaps the most brilliant, and certainly the most colorful, of Indiana's war leaders was John T. Wilder. A young machinist and engineer from Greensburg, he enlisted in an Indiana volunteer regiment as a private. He rose from the ranks to become a brigadier general. Assigned to the senseless task of

GEN. LEW WALLACE of Crawfordsville (mounted) and his men entered the war clad in dazzling Zouave uniforms. Wallace was twelve hours late bringing his men to the front at the bloody battle of Shiloh, and General Grant never let him command in the field again. (Leslie's)

INDIANA SOLDIERS and the steamships which plied the Ohio River are well-represented in this scene at Vicksburg, Mississippi, where the steamers, guarded here by an iron-clad gunboat, were used as transports. (Leslie's)

chasing General Morgan's superb Kentucky cavalry with his infantry regiment, his engineering mind went to work. He and his men stole enough fine Kentucky mounts from enemy camps and Kentucky farms to convert his unit into "Mounted Infantry," without one cent of cost to the government for mounts or accoutrements, as Leslie's history of the war states.

Not yet satisfied, he wangled the first consignment of the brand-new Spencer rifles. The first repeating weapon ever used in warfare, it was a carbine known to the troops as the "Seven-Shooter." Moving very fast and "going into battle, firing faster than man ever fired before," as one of his men wrote, Wilder was the true inventor of the "blitzkrieg." With such speed and firepower, the Union generals called on Wilder's "Lightning Brigade," wherever it was, to stop Confederate breakthroughs, to flank the enemy line, or to head off enemy advances. At Chickamauga, he and Gen. George H. Thomas, "The Rock of Chickamauga," saved the Union defeat from becoming a total disaster. Today, a 92-foot tower of Georgia limestone, built with funds donated by his own men, is the most imposing monument in the National Military Park on the battle site.

[65]

THIS MILITARY COMMISSION sat in judgment at Indianapolis during the famous "treason trials." Accused were the Knights of the Golden Circle, a secret organization of Confederate sympathizers, estimated by some to have had 50,000 members in Indiana. Dr. William A. Bowles, who built the French Lick Hotel, Lambdin P. Milligan, and others among its leaders were convicted by the commission. (ISL)

"THE GENERAL," now at Kennesaw, Georgia, is a much visited memento of the Civil War, thanks to the exploits of a spy named Andrews from Ohio and his men, including Hoosiers. Their feat of derring-do that captured this Confederate locomotive behind the lines in Georgia, has been made immortal by Walt Disney in *The Great Locomotive Chase*. The exploit met disaster near Ringgold, Georgia. Several of the men were hanged as spies.

INDIANA'S STATEHOUSE was draped in black crepe as Lincoln's body lay in state there before burial in Springfield, Illinois on April 30, 1865. (ISL)

Indiana from 1866 to 1900

HOOSIERS SIGHED with relief and rejoicing when the news came that Lee had surrendered at Appomattox. But the rejoicing was short-lived. As the aftermath of the nation's greatest loss, a train rolled into Indianapolis with the body of one of its own on April 30. On horseback, in buggies and wagons, and afoot, Hoosiers streamed to the statehouse where Lincoln's body lay in state.

Peace brought an end to the war-induced bustle. Hoosiers went on clearing the land in northern Indiana, and farming was the main occupation. However, Chicago and smaller cities needed lumber for building, the people needed wagons, buggies and carriages, and they could afford furniture. The giant Indiana hardwood trees, which the earliest settlers had burned as they cleared the land, were hauled by ox-team. and rail to hundreds of sawmills in the state. All sorts of woodworking industries, making everything from fine furniture to prairie schooners, ladders, and churns sprang up.

The hardwood lumbering era was an era as important and bustling as the pine epoch in Michigan and New England. But without "white water" and Paul Bunyan, it lacked the glamor. Its history has never been written, but it is noteworthy that the magnificent forests of Indiana—maple and walnut, tulip and cherry, placed it first of all the states in production of hardwood lumber by 1890. Virtually every little town had a woodworking industry, with handy Indiana farm boys learning craftsmanship by the hand-methods used.

In 1868, James Oliver, a South Bend man, invented a chilled-steel plow. It was the first plow that would satisfactorily cut and turn the prairie sod and other heavy soils. Cyrus McCormick, an imaginative farm youth from Virginia, produced a successful reaper which allowed one man with a team of horses to cut and bind grain, while earlier it had taken many men to do the same task. His method of selling his reaper to Midwest farmers was also somewhat of an innovation: for $10 down and the balance after the harvest, this time-and-labor-saving device could be had by any farmer. His sales were so large in the Midwest that he moved his factory from Virginia to Chicago in 1845.

County agricultural societies to promote better varieties of grains, pureblooded stock, and the new farm machines were formed. The Indiana State Fair, founded in 1852, spread the gospel of better farming. Purdue University, the state's Land Grant College, was founded in 1872. Soon, it was showing new methods to farmers at short courses on the campus and Farmers Institutes in their home communities.

Education in Indiana had been haphazard, with no provision for compulsory attendance and no tax money allotted for public schools until the Constitution of 1852. Universal school education became the rule after the Civil War, and every remote community had its own tax-supported one- or two-room school. Imaginative Hoosiers found the school names such as "District No. 4" monotonous, and bestowed on each a distinctive name, based on local lore. Typical names of Hoosier schools attended by some of our oldest citizens of today were "Hardscrabble," "Hanging Tree," "Sauerkraut," "Bloody Corners," "Crane Heaven," "Frog Hollow."

Pioneer institutions of higher learning flourished as the century advanced. Academies and small normal schools were established in many communities to provide teachers and preparation for college. New colleges were founded. In 1897, the Legislature made education compulsory.

Indiana still was predominantly agricultural, but it experienced in the last two decades of the century a boom reminiscent of the Gold Rush and Cattle Drives farther west. An Ohio State geologist had once stated conclusively that the Trenton rock formation underlying most of Indiana and Ohio could not possibly contain gas and oil. Oil men had, therefore, studiously avoided drilling in the area, until test-drilling near Lima, Ohio, proved the geologist wrong.

The frenzy of wildcatting that followed revealed the greatest discovery of an oil and gas field ever until Spindletop and the East Texas field. Starting in Ohio, the drilling spread westward into Indiana, to develop into what became known as the Lima-Indiana field. The first Indiana gas was discovered at Portland in 1886, and the first producing oil well came in in Wells County in 1889.

Thousands of wells were drilled during the next decade. Gas was produced in prodigal quantities, half of which was wasted by burning at the well head or simply by escaping into the air. Not knowing what else to do with it, enterprising communities offered the gas free of charge to eastern industries as fuel for their factories. East Central Indiana became a boom area.

THOMAS ALVA EDISON was a roving teen-age telegrapher who got fired many times. Dismissed at Adrian,
Michigan, he moved on to Fort Wayne during the Civil
War, and was fired again. In 1864, he went to Indianapolis to work as a second-class operator for Western Union,
and there he perfected the first of more than two thousand inventions—a device that would repeat and slow
down Morse-code messages, making the telegrapher's
work less difficult. His fellow employees nevertheless
thought that the future great inventor was an "odd
duck," and he was fired again after a few months and
moved on to Cincinnati.

NOTRE DAME Catholic School at South Bend had become a university, but had never heard of collegiate football when this print was made soon after the end of the Civil War. The twin-spired church
at the left and the administration building with its famous golden dome still stand.

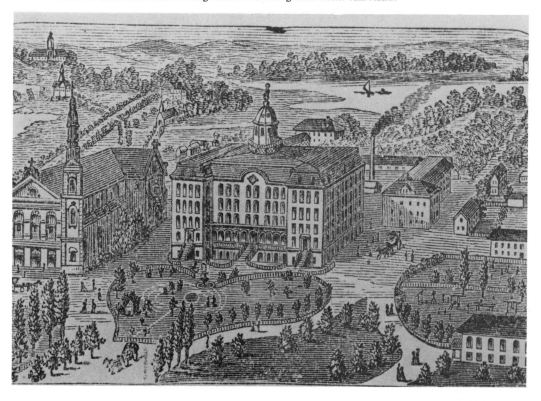

[69]

INDIANA STATE NORMAL SCHOOL was established at Terre Haute in 1886 after the state accepted the offer of the community to donate the Vigo County Seminary (shown about that time) and $50,000 to establish the first school to train teachers in the state. (ISU)

ASBURY COLLEGE and most of its campus at Greencastle during the 1870s: This institution sponsored by the Methodist Episcopal Church and devoted mainly to training ministers grew to be DePauw University.

ONE OF THE GREATEST inventions for farming was the Oliver chilled-steel plow, invented by James Oliver of South Bend in 1868. It was a favorite of the sod-busters who helped conquer the trans-Mississippi West. This photograph is believed to show the original plow in use in St. Joseph County. (NIHS)

SCHUYLER COLFAX, a South Bend editor, served as speaker of the house during the Civil War. In 1868 he was elected vice president as a Republican under Grant, but suspicion of involvement in the Credit Mobilier fraud—the Watergate of the nineteenth century—ruined his political career, although no guilt was proven. (NIHS)

Glass factories by the score moved from the East or were started anew, among them by the Ball Brothers, who located at Muncie. Sleepy rural villages became boom towns—the little town of Matthews with a population of 627 in 1970, supported 19 saloons, and for one year, a major league baseball team. As the wildcatters drilled, restaurants stayed open 24 hours a day—one operator even threw away the front-door key.

Oil company promoters ran excursion trains from the East to the fields for prospective buyers of their stock, which was not always the golden opportunity that was advertised. Such towns as Portland, Muncie, Anderson, Marion, Kokomo, New Castle, Elwood, and Alexandria boomed and became industrialized cities. Peak gas production of $7,000,000 per year was reached by the opening of the twentieth century. Oil production, with new discoveries in southwestern Indiana, has since totaled more than 400,000,000 barrels. The extraction methods of the time were wasteful, though, and the production of both gas and oil tapered off rapidly soon after 1900. It was, nevertheless, great while it lasted, and the state made substantial industrial gains.

[71]

Agriculture, however, continued to dominate the state's economy at the turn of the century. There were 222,000 farms, with about 750,000 of the state's population living and most of them working on the farm, while factory employment totaled only 176,227 in 1904.

Considering its size, the state's production of basic farm crops from the Civil War to the present has been phenomenal. For much of the late 1800s, it was second or third in the production of wheat. Recently, its production of hogs is exceeded only by Iowa. In corn, its total production usually is in the top three or four states. The Pioneer Hybrid Seed Co. of Iowa ran a scientific study to determine the one area east of the Mississippi least subject to crop failure, when locating its eastern production facilities. The Tipton-Flora locations in north Central Indiana, in the incredibly fertile, well-watered Tipton Till Plain, which covers a third of the state, was chosen as the most suitable.

The surge of economic activity during and after the Civil War also created a demand for culture in the form of books, art, and music.

Although there had been struggling writers of merit before, Edward Eggleston of Vevay; James Whitcomb Riley, a Greenfield native; and Lew Wallace of Crawfordsville were the first Hoosiers to gain national recognition. It brought all of them great rewards, even financially. Riley extolled the virtues of the idyllic Hoosier rural life—when rural and small town boys skinny-dipped in the "Old Swimmin' Hole" and "The frost was on the punkin and the fodder was in the shock." According to David Randall, director of the Lilly Library, Riley received $2,000,000 from sale of his poems. No poet ever so captured the hearts and pocketbooks of the American people.

Lew Wallace, the swashbuckling drillmaster, politician, and lawyer bungled his syntax but had a sure sense of drama. His novel *Ben Hur* was easily the best-selling American book of the nineteenth century. Placed on the stage by Erlanger in 1900 with the chariots racing furiously on a stage treadmill, it played many hundred performances. With two movie box-office hit versions, *Ben Hur* may well be the all-time favorite American drama.

Following the footsteps of George Winter, Lewis Peckham, Marcus Mote, Jacob Cox, and other pioneers who often turned to barn and sign painting, the ante-bellum prosperity enabled would-be Indiana artists to study in Europe or in the art centers of the East. William Meritt Chase, Otto Stark. T. C. Steele, J. Ottis Adams, William Forsyth, and Homer Davisson were among those winning national recognition. The picturesque and backward areas of South Central Indiana were favorite locations for their talented easels. They became known nationally as the "Brown County School."

Musical entertainment in Indiana was long limited to the fiddle and drum for dances, a rare piano in Ohio River mansions, and plain song in churches. Probably the first noteworthy advance in music came in the 1840s with the

SOUTHERN INDIANA boasts several noted caves and natural curiosities. Thousands have visited Jug Rock, a mushroom shape carved by water action out of the limestone of Martin County, near Shoals. It has become the center of a popular park for picnickers, many of whose names are carved on the sixty-foot-high phenomenon. In this cavern-ridden area there are many legends about the Knights of the Golden Circle, horse thieves, highwaymen, moonshiners, and buried treasure. (ISL)

THE LUMBERING BOOM, which followed the Civil War in northern Indiana, led to the establishment of hundreds of sawmills and woodworking industries. This Marshall County planing mill flourished in the 1880s.

arrival of large groups of German immigrants, who introduced folk and art music of the choral variety with their "Sängerbund" choral groups as well as the men's choruses of their gymnastics clubs known as "Turnvereins."

The Civil War introduced band music to many communities, large and small. Elkhart pioneered a new industry for the state when Charles Girard Conn began producing cornets in 1875. He started a campaign to organize bands and orchestras in all American schools, and Elkhart became the band-instrument capital of the United States.

Social distinction began to be more pronounced. While in the past farmer, businessmen, and small industrialists had been united by common interests, their increasingly divergent interests served to divide them. Farmers complained about being overcharged by businessmen, railroads, and others; businessmen complained about industry; and labor grew restive and felt exploited by industry.

The National Grange for farmers first appeared in 1871 near Terre Haute. Originally a social and educational organization, it soon became a political force that agitated for more legislators from rural areas, reduction of freight rates, and relief from excessive taxation of real estate. The movement began rapidly and became powerful on a national basis.

Labor began to complain of injustices. The Knights of Labor, an early union that had come into the state in the 1870s, was declining in power. In a meeting in 1881 in Terre Haute, a center for growing coal mining and railroad shops that seemed to generate liberal leaders, labor officials called for a better structured organization than the Knights of Labor, and five years later the American Federation of Labor was formed.

In 1894, after one of the great financial panics, Eugene V. Debs, a lifelong Terre Haute resident, organized the American Railway Union, which included all classes of rail workers. Debs who spent a great deal of his life in jail for his labor activities and liberal political views, also organized in 1901 the Socialist Party in Indianapolis. Debs was a dirty name to much of the Indiana and American establishment in the late 1800s and early 1900s, but today most Hoosiers unite in honoring him as one of the state's heroes.

He was the Socialist Party candidate for president in 1904, 1908, 1912, and 1920. In his last race, he polled nearly a million votes, although he was serving time in federal prison for opposing World War I.

THE EXPOSITION BUILDING near present Meridian Street in downtown Indianapolis replaced Camp Morton, the Civil War mustering and training camp. Shown as it was about 1870, it became the permanent site of the Indiana State Fair which, before the war, was held in a different city each year. (ISL)

PASADENA—"THE INDIANA COLONY:" Hoosier lore forgotten by most includes the fact that the granddaddy of all football-bowl-game parades was started by Indianans. Pasadena was founded by a group of migrating Hoosiers, who purchased a large California tract once occupied by the San Gabriel mission, founded in 1771. The official name of the town was "The Indiana Colony" until the name was changed to Pasadena in 1875. This nineteenth-century parade entry pales beside today's floats, but the roses were real and the unidentified belles possess old-time Hoosier charm. (Woodson)

THE SINGER SEWING
Machine Company, whose employees posed outside the firm's plant in the 1870s *(left)* was to become world famous, and its salesmen scurried all over the globe to convince Zulus, Seminoles, Hindus, Arabs, Australian aborigines, and denizens of the Amazon jungles that the Singer product was preferable to tedious hand-sewing—and they had remarkable success. The lithograph (*below*) was issued by the company in 1892. (NIHS)

ZULULAND

STOVEPIPE HATS still adorned upper-class young blades at South Bend when Albert McDonald took this photograph in 1872. The men's identities are unknown, but several undoubtedly became very important. (NIHS)

THERE WERE FEW ROADS so rutted and muddy that the horse-drawn circus could not use them and virtually every backroads hamlet had exciting entertainment at least once a year. This is the band-wagon of a "15-and-25-cent" show. (ISL)

LA PORTE BUSINESS CAME to a standstill along one of its main streets when the circus parade passed by in the morning to advertise the coming performance. (LPHS)

WASHINGTON STREET in Indianapolis in 1874, looking west from Meridian, shows ladies with bustles, parasols, and fashionable gowns competing for the right-of-way with a diverse assortment of horse-drawn and hand-pushed vehicles. (ISL)

FRENCH LICK SPRINGS HOTEL grew to be one of the great watering places of America in the 1870s. This view shows it after it had been enlarged to 1,000 rooms and 25 acres of floor space, in the midst of 4,000 beautiful acres of grounds. Monon Railroad trains brought the affluent from all parts of America and abroad to relax and sample its medicinal waters, whose virtues seem to have been mainly those of a laxative. (Sheraton)

RIVALING "INDY 500" and the Kentucky Derby, steamboat races provided the most famous speed contest of the 1800s when the *Robert E. Lee* raced the *Natchez* for supremacy of the river. Hoosiers had a special interest in the race since the *Lee* was built in 1866 at the Hill and Roberts yards in New Albany. In December 1870, the *Lee* sank near New Orleans, and the Howard Shipyards at New Albany built a new hull for the queen of the river. (ISL)

[79]

THE STEAMBOAT STILL REIGNED along the Ohio River's shores in the late 1800s. These packets are unloading at the Madison wharf boat. (ISL)

THE SIDEWHEELER *Louisville* passes Aurora, one of the oldest cities on the river, whose prosperity hinged on the river traffic.

INDIANA'S RIVER CITIES had mansions that were unexcelled in grace and elegance in the deep South, the result of wealth accumulated in the Ohio-Mississippi rivers trade and the services of such fine architects as Thomas Costigan. Hillforest, the home shown, was built in antebellum days on the hill above Aurora by a wealthy steamboat captain. It survives today, its furnishings restored, as a historical landmark open to the public. (ISL)

THE HOWARD SHIPYARDS at new Albany built some of the most famous boats on the river in the halcyon days of steam. After a century of service, it was still operated during World War II to build landing craft and other vessels for the U. S. Navy. (ISL)

COMPETITION FROM TRAINS and river barges brought a radical change in steamboat styles on the Ohio and Mississippi. When the huge cotton-hauling sidewheelers found big cargoes scarcer, owners went to a much smaller, shallow-draft sternwheeler, such as the *Sprague*, for use on the smaller rivers. The *Sprague* may have served as a tugboat. (ISL)

JAMES D. "BLUE JEANS" WILLIAMS, a "dirt farmer" from near Vincennes who had a pioneer background with little schooling, was popular with Indiana voters. In 1876, he ran for governor against the sophisticated Benjamin Harrison, who derisively nicknamed him "Blue Jeans" because he wore his accustomed homespun garb while campaigning. The term backfired on Harrison, however, when the voters, most of whom wore blue jeans, butternut, coonskin, or other pioneer garb, elected Williams. Williams, next to the oxen, is shown speaking at a logrolling. (ISL)

CUSTER'S LAST STAND in 1876 was one of the most awesome American tragedies of the nineteenth century. The North Indiana Historical Society at South Bend kept the long-haired general's memory ever green for visitors to its museum with this life-size wax effigy. (NIHS)

SAM, PETE AND MAX STAR CLOTHING was a Fort Wayne firm that was not the least bashful about letting the consumer know of its existence. Horsecars in the 1870s brought patrons to the store and to buy Kentucky liquors, Red Front chewing tobacco, and other goods, on the east side of Calhoun, between Main and Columbia. (FWPL)

THE DAYS OF STEAM were important in Indiana when this photo was taken around 1880. (ISL)

MARCEAU & POWER located at 36-38 N. Illinois Street in Indianapolis, trusted the artist and lithographer more than their own work to advertise the photo "salon" in the 1870s. Note the simplified spelling of "fotografers" that was used by them long before the *Chicago Tribune* launched its spelling campaign. (ISL)

THIS LITTLE BEAUTY from Vevay has no inkling in 1880 that the bisque doll she holds will be an antique worth a fortune in her great-granddaughter's time. (ISL)

ISN'T SHE SPLENDIFEROUS? This young lady must have had Hoosier tongues wagging when she visited Indianapolis with her husband in September 1880. P. T. Barnum, the greatest showman of the century, was then seventy, and had married a young chick, the daughter of an English associate, John Fish. It seems unlikely that Mrs. Barnum would let herself be outshone by any of the spangled beauties in the Barnum shows. (ISL)

Old Salem Church.
Built, 1840.

OLD SALEM CHURCH, a Brethren log edifice built in the country somewhere near Greensburg in 1840, was still in use at the time this congregation was photographed around 1880. There still are similar log churches, now covered with clapboards, in some southern Indiana communities today.

INDIANA HAD COAL in great beds in the southwest part of the state, but little of it was mined until about 1880, as wood was plentiful and cheap. This is the tipple of the Standard deep mine. (ISL)

LIKE PANCAKES AND SYRUP, carriages and horseshoes go together. The Wm. C. Pittner Carriage Shop is at the left in this LaPorte scene. (LPHS)

THE STUDEBAKER COMPANY still meant "wagon works" in the 1880s. These are the workmen at the main plant in South Bend at that time. The growing firm induced many Poles to immigrate to the city, who became the pioneers of the state's largest Polish-American community today. (NIHS)

ONE OF SOUTH BEND'S first frame houses was this one at 117 Lincolnway East, built in 1831 by Benjamin Coquillard. It was used around 1880 as the Union Hall Tavern. (NIHS)

THE C. L. CENTLIVRE BEER GARDEN, next to the brewery and residence of the owner on the St. Joseph River, was a popular watering place in Fort Wayne in the 1880s. (FWPL)

THE DEFEAT of presidential candidate Harrison caused little sorrow in Brown County in 1884. Most natives were hereditary Democrats who rejoiced with their only newspaper that the "Augean Stable" was going to be cleaned out by their favorite, Grover Cleveland. (Lilly)

INDIANA STATE NORMAL COLLEGE was mighty proud of the first building constructed on its Terre Haute campus in 1870 (above). The lower photo shows curiosity-seekers viewing the ruins of the structure after it was destroyed in a disastrous fire on April 9, 1888. The school is now known as Indiana State University. (ISU)

[88]

INDIANA STATE UNIVERSITY'S second building was erected in 1888 to replace the structure which burned on the Terre Haute campus. It was razed in 1950. (ISU)

THESE BADGES AND UNIFORMS were in keeping with the authority held by the Vincennes police force in 1884. The chief and assistant chief (with campaign hats in front row) could well be mistaken for Union Army generals or frontier marshals. (V. U.)

IN VICTORIAN TIMES, a girl could get attention, admiring glances, or jealous looks with the help of her milliner and papa's or hubby's cash. This unknown beauteous belle is from LaPorte, about 1890. (ISL)

THE DAPPER DRUMMER from the city was a glamorous figure to small-town Indiana girls in horse-and-buggy days as he alighted from the train and visited the stores, "drumming up business." This one, unidentified, probably has his samples in the square valise and his extra shirts and celluloid collars in the other.

[89]

BASEBALL WAS THE FIRST organized sport at Indiana State Normal School in Terre Haute (now Indiana State University). Handlebar mustaches and derby hats were all the rage. (ISU)

THESE YOUNG FORT WAYNE art students, posed in 1890, are believed to be a student group from the original Fort Wayne Art Society. Seated right is Alice Diggins Mahurin, and seated left, Lou Wiley. The others are unknown. (FWHS)

BRAVE FIREMEN of Engine House No. 2 in Fort Wayne with their equipment, pictured in 1889: At left is a horse reel wagon; at right the controversial Silsboy "Anthony Wayne" fire wagon. (FWHS)

FIRE CHIEF HENRY HILBRECHT of Fort Wayne (seated) was photographed in his official chief's buggy in 1889. Too bad that the picture wasn't in living color, since the freshly-swabbed buggy undoubtedly was fire-wagon red. (FWHS)

MEN WORE LEOTARDS in the late 1800s as this picture of the LaPorte Fire Department running hose team shows. Note the sprinting position of some of the fleet runners who pulled the hose cart instead of relying on horses. (LPHS)

NORTHERN INDIANA PROVIDED a large part of the lumber which built the growing cities of the Great Lakes area, including Chicago and Milwaukee. This is the harbor at Michigan City near the end of the 1800s. (FMNB)

[92]

THE DRAY-FOR-HIRE was an essential service for pickups and deliveries for most merchants, since few had their own teams. This picture seems to have been taken in Kosciusko County in the 1890s.

GAS FLAMBEAUX made the "Crossroads of America" a livelier and safer place at night during the late 1880s and early 1890s, when natural gas was piped to Indianapolis from newly-discovered wells. The structure at right in this East Market Street scene appears to be an opera house. (ISL)

COTTON MANUFACTURE, for which steamboats provided cheap transportation in the 1800s, was important to several Ohio River cities. This is a view of the Evansville Cotton Mills in 1889. (ECC)

NEAR THE CENTURY'S END, Indiana had several medical schools. This is the class of 1898 at the Fort Wayne College of Medicine as they were in November 1895. (FWHS)

HOPE HOSPITAL'S nursing staff in Fort Wayne at the turn of the century: The lone male is Dr. Dancer, also of the hospital staff. (FWHS)

THE SOUTH BEND High School Class of 1892 posed for this group picture. (NIHS)

OLD SOLDIERS' REUNION at Cannelton, probably in 1895: Union Army veterans had a strong esprit de corps, despite transportation difficulties. As their ranks dwindled, community respect deepened, while many of the reminiscences of their part in the war were embellished with age. (ISL)

[95]

INDIANAPOLIS WAS HOST to the national convention of the Grand Army of the Republic in 1893— surely a stirring occasion. Headquarters was the G.A.R. "flagship" *Kearsage* on the Indiana statehouse lawn. Note the many-armed telephone posts. (ISL)

ELWOOD HAYNES of Kokomo with the gasoline-powered auto-buggy he invented posed in 1894 alongside the marker commemorating his first successful run at seven miles per hour on the Pumpkin-vine Pike in Howard County. On its return run to the city, the new-fangled monster came over a rise in the road into a bevy of young girls on bicycles. They scattered like frightened pigeons before the on-slaught of a falcon. (ISL)

INDIANAPOLIS PARTISANS claimed that C. D. Black, a prosperous bicycle dealer of that city, invented a successful gas-powered automobile in 1891, three years before Haynes' vehicle. Others said that he only took apart a Daimler-Benz car he had imported from Germany that year, duplicated it part for part, and added a buggy-whip. Here he is shown seated in his controversial car before the Benjamin Harrison monument on the Statehouse lawn in 1920. (ISL)

HORSES MAY HAVE still dominated Indiana transportation and power as the 1900s began, but Apperson and Haynes already were manufacturing automobiles. More than 200 Indiana firms would produce their makes of automobiles in a few years.

The Munsen Company of LaPorte was one of the earliest, starting manufacture of the strange contraptions shown in 1898. Two of the firm's models are shown, adorned by venturesome ladies of the town, with male chauffeurs. Note the sunshade which has been added for their comfort in the photograph above. (LPHS)

WHO SAYS ELECTRIC AUTOS are not practical? The Waverly Company of Indianapolis, which claimed to be the world's largest manufacturer of bicycles, turned to auto-making, among the very first in the United States, in 1898, making the Waverly Electric auto. It had bicycle wheels and a storage battery to operate the electric motor. Obvious advantages over the gasoline-motor cars advertised by the company which survived nearly twenty years were silent operation, ease of maintenance, and the fact that they were not nearly so likely to scare horses. Little old ladies of Indianapolis still were driving Waverlys in the 1930s. Note the primitive truck in this 1915 showroom scene. (ISL)

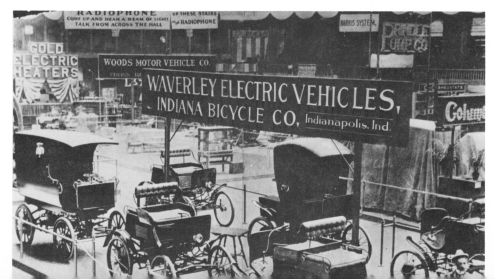

AN INDIANAPOLIS CYCLING CLUB chose the Indiana statehouse steps during a quiet Sunday time to be photographed about 1895 with their prized high-wheeled "bone-breaker" mounts. (ISL)

THE BICYCLING CRAZE was near its peak on September 4, 1899, when Sarah Frose posed with her wheels in this idyllic rural setting in Allen County. Women's styles were becoming more functional so that they could participate in this form of recreation. (FWHS)

HANGING ROCK DAIRY near Indianapolis dispensed milk directly from the can into the customer's pail, unpasteurized, unhomogenized, and unbottled. If this seems archaic and unsanitary, consider that in much of the world the milkman used a burro and goatskin bags during the late 1800s. (ISL)

THE SUNNY SIDE SALOON, somewhere in Indianapolis, at the turn of the century. (ISL)

POP AND MOM GROCERY in Indianapolis with Pop and Mom in front of the store. Perishable citrus being scarce and expensive, "fresh fruit" was pretty much limited to bananas and apples. (ISL)

A THRESHING SCENE at Andrews Farm near
LaPorte in the late 1800s: The wheeled traction engine not only provided power on the
spot to operate the threshing separator, but
pulled the machine from farm to farm during
late summer. (NIHS)

MILLER'S MEAT MARKET displayed sides
of beef outside their store in LaPorte during
cool weather. (LPHS)

HOME BUTCHERING and slaughter by pro-
prietors of butcher shops was common in the
late 1800s in Indiana, despite the fact that the
large slaughterhouses were maintained at Indianapolis, Fort Wayne, the Ohio River towns,
and elsewhere. Performed in the winter, the
work eliminated spoilage problems before re-
frigeration was available. The man in the center, T. H. Hamilton, had butcher shops at
several locations in the state at various times.
(ISL)

BARR STREET FARMERS MARKET in Fort Wayne is a very old institution, dating back to ante-
bellum days. It occupied various sites until it moved to this spot. Produce wagons parked under the
trees, where fruit, vegetables, and shoppers got the benefit of the shade—even if the horses did not
(above). Later, a roofed shelter *(below)* was set up to even better protect the produce and the customers. (FWHS–FWPL)

THE ACHDUTH VESHALOM SYNA-gogue at the southwest corner of West Wayne and Harrison streets in Fort Wayne has been razed and replaced by the Central Building. (FWPL)

PETER ECKRICH & SONS of Fort Wayne started as small meat packers in the late 1800s and grew in size with their reputation for sausage specialties. John Eckrich, oldest son of the founder, drove the first and only delivery vehicle of the firm when the picture was taken in the late 1890s. (FWHS)

IF TODAY'S BASEBALL SALARIES had prevailed eighty years ago, America might have lost one of its most popular writers. Ohio-born Zane Grey, author of countless best-selling western novels, came to Fort Wayne about 1895, after starring at the University of Pennsylvania, to play with these early pro devotees of Abner Doubleday's new sport. (FWHS)

CALHOUN STREET in Fort Wayne looked like this as the 1900s dawned. The scene looks to the
north toward Berry. Just beyond the dog is a Herman Berghoff Brewery wagon; the top floor of the
building at the extreme left carries the symbolic sign of Sion S. Bass Post 40 (G.A.R.). Just beyond the
C & D sign on right is the famous Aveline Hotel, later destroyed in a tragic fire. (FWHS)

BANJO MUSIC provided entertainment for these black patrons of a popular tavern on Poke Street in South Bend, the site of latter-day Spiro's Department Store. The group was photographed around the turn of century. (NIHS)

THE FAMOUS KANKAKEE MARSHES were being drained rapidly at the end of the century, but they still teemed with game, and were a favorite rendezvous of hunters. Tenting on the banks of the river is this party from South Bend and vicinity, with Dr. H. T. Montgomery at the rear. (NIHS)

TALKING MOTION PICTURES as we know them had their advent in 1927 with Al Jolson in Warner Brothers' *The Jazz Singer*. We can't describe what kind were shown in this Wabash carnival attraction at the turn of century, but perhaps accompaniment for the primitive flickers came through the morning glory horn of an Edison Gramophone. (ISL)

The Twentieth Century: 1900 to 1950

AS THE TWENTIETH CENTURY opened in Indiana, the hard times and the political unrest of the 1890s faded into the background. The state was rapidly changing from agricultural to industrial. Brash young men with creative ideas started careers that would make them tycoons.

One typical example is Carl Fisher, a grade-school dropout and teenage bicycle salesman in Indianapolis, who became a multimillionaire starting out with an automobile agency. Fisher joined in 1904 with James Allison (who was to become the largest airplane manufacturer during World War II) in buying the patent for an acetylene lamp for automobile headlights from a French inventor who had been unable to find a buyer. Their newly-founded Prest-o-Lite company made millions, and a few years later they sold out to Union Carbide.

Fisher's promotional abilities knew few limits. In 1909, he built the Indianapolis Speedway and promoted the first Indianapolis 500 race. In 1912, he started a promotion which resulted in the building of the first transcontinental road—the Lincoln Highway.

A year later, he invested in a desert island off the coast near Miami, Florida, and started his greatest promotion—the building and sale of Miami Beach. Then in 1915, he promoted the construction of the Dixie Highway that was to carry Midwesterners to his new development in Florida. The result was probably the greatest real estate coup of all time.

But Fisher also made mistakes that are seldom remembered today. His Prest-o-Lite factory blew up, killing many workers, whereupon it had to move out of the city of Indianapolis. His first Indianapolis 500 race ended at 300 miles after several drivers were killed in accidents caused by the buckling

MANY FINE MANSIONS graced West Berry Street in Fort Wayne at the turn of the century. This imposing home, at the corner of that street and Lafayette, was built by Franklin P. Randall, who served five terms as mayor of the city, including the Civil War period. He was a lawyer who became a real estate and railroad magnate in the late 1800s. (FWPL)

asphalt track. His biggest mistake came in the mid-1920s. Emboldened by his sensational success in Florida, he started to develop Montauk, Long Island, as the "Miami Beach of the North." The Florida bubble burst, the Depression hit, and by 1932 Fisher had lost virtually everything, including Montauk.

Allison, on the other hand, went on to make a fortune building automobile engines and later airplane engines. In World War II, Allison's company in Indianapolis was the largest manufacturer of military aircraft engines.

During the early years of the century, the final touches were put on draining the vast marshes of the Kankakee which for more than 200 years was one of the greatest game preserves of America. Farmers also fenced and plowed much of the once open-range cattle country of the western Indiana prairies.

By 1920, ninety-one percent of the state's land was cleared and in farm production. Natural fertility of the soil along with an ideal climate induced food processing companies to locate their plants in Indiana. For a good many years, Indiana (especially in Grant, Tipton, and Howard Counties) produced

L. STRAUSS & CO. was one of three or four stores which set style trends in Indiand in the same way Marshall Field & Co. did in Chicago. No stark functional storefront would do, and the stone-sculptured one of Strauss on Washington Street in Indianapolis (between Illinois and Meridian) at the turn of the century was something to make Phidias and Praxiteles wonder. (ISL)

PLANETTE LUMBER COMPANY offices in LaPorte around 1900: Note the great assortment of picture frames, for Grandpa's or Grandma's enlarged portrait. (LPHS)

more than one-fourth of all the tomatoes for canning and catsup-making in the United States. It was easily first in the production of mint oil, and later also in popcorn.

The early 1900s were exciting times in Indiana as the state moved rapidly from a mostly-rural to an industrial economy. The "gas and oil boom" of the 1880s and 1900s was followed by the explosive growth of automobile manufacturing in the state, and by an incredible expansion in transportation caused by the development of electric streetcars into cross-country trains that would compete with steam trains.

A prime mover in this matter was a Hoosier attorney, Charles L. Henry, who coined the term "Interurban." He described his idea of electric interurban trains at the Chicago World's Fair of 1893. Probably the first such line was an eighteen-mile track built out of Portland, Oregon, that year. In Indiana, it began with an eight-mile track from Indianapolis to a popular amusement and picnic park at nearby Broad Ripple.

The idea was slow in catching on until the early 1900s, when it soon became a craze, especially in the Midwest. By the 1920s, more than 18,000 miles of track had been laid in the United States. Of these, 2,000 were in Indiana, more than ten percent of the total. Indianapolis was known as the "Interurban Capital of the World." Twelve major electric railways ran out of the city. The world's largest Interurban terminal was built in Indianapolis in 1904 on West Market Street, only two blocks from the "Crossroads of America." It consisted of what was then an ultra-modern office building, adjoining a cavernous nine-track train shed that could accommodate thirty Interurban trains at once.

At its zenith in 1914, before World War I slowed down the activity, the interurbans brought seven million people, twice the population of the state, into the terminal each year. Speculation was rampant as new lines were built. Fort Wayne was second to Indianapolis as an interurban center, and there were thirty companies operating or planning to operate in Allen County alone.

Competition of the automobile began to be felt, and small towns who gloried in the easiest and best public transportation they ever had, began to lose their service in the 1920s. The Union Traction Company merged with many of the troubled lines, but others still remained profitable. The end came with the 1929 stock market crash.

Samuel Insull and Samuel Insull, Jr., the utility magnates, headed the Indiana Railroad Company, organized in 1930, which took over the defunct Union Traction Company in an attempt to save a good part of its business. Although the company went into receivership in 1933, it continued in operation until 1941.

Probably the worst interurban wreck happened on September 21, 1910,

A GRUESOME MYSTERY lurks behind the motherly portrait of Belle Gunness and her little brood. She is believed to have lured to her LaPorte farm thirteen well-to-do men with cash or sizable insurance policies which were converted to her name. They were attracted by matrimonial agency advertising—and they soon disappeared from sight after spending a few days at the farm. When a hired farmhand exposed her in 1902, digging started and bodies were found all around. Soon after, her house burned to the ground, and in the ashes were three skeletons of children and a headless woman, who, it is said, was much too small to be Belle. Those who knew her insisted they saw her the next year in California. The trio of children shown were adopted by her. (LPHS)

EQUINE ARISTOCRATS were the fire horses. They are shown with the gallant fire laddies and equipment at the Indianapolis Fire Department headquarters at the southwest corner of Massachusetts and New York about 1900. (ISL)

[109]

AARON McCORMICK, the oldest surviving original settler of Indianapolis, was honored in this picture taken at Old Settler's Day in 1902.

CAPS REPLACED stovepipe hats in 1900 when these three members of the South Bend Cycle Club posed with their wheels. (NIHS)

"GAS BELT CHAMPIONS" was the title of the small-town high-school football team from Pendleton in 1905. The Gas Belt, a rather indefinite area of north-central Indiana, definitely included such major cities as Muncie and Anderson. (ISC)

INDIANA STATE NORMAL School, now I.S.U., at Terre Haute had football as its second varsity sport in the early 1900s. This is the 1902 Varsity Team. (ISU)

when a steel car and a wooden one carrying passengers to the Allen County Fair collided head-on. Forty-one persons were killed by the terrific impact.

Indiana's weather has a habit of going occasionally berserk—creating sensational headlines about tornadoes, floods, bitter cold, drought, tropical heat, or fierce gales on Lake Michigan. According to nautical authorities, storm-tossed Lake Michigan is as dangerous as an angry Atlantic. Hundreds of sailors have lost their lives on the lake, from the crew of Sieur de la Salle's ship *Griffon* which was mysteriously lost with all hands on the Great Lakes in the 1600s, to those who suffered from the raging storm on Armistice Day, November 11, 1948.

Graham Hutton, a discerning Britisher, spent seven years in the Midwest. He then wrote, in 1944, one of the most interesting, controversial, and possibly most objective books about Indiana. The Midwest, he wrote, has wider and more violent extremes of weather than any place on the face of the globe, except for some parts of the interior of Russia.

Perhaps he was not far from wrong, although it might be hard to get any Chamber-of-Commerce secretary to admit it. There was the awful winter of 1917, a dreadful memory to those now living who recall the blizzards and the twenty-degree-below weather that brought nearly all activity to a standstill for many days on end, except for the battle of survival, and to keep warm. Then there was March 1913, when a terrific storm was spawned in the western plains. Tornadoes created havoc in Omaha. The storms reached Indiana and Ohio without letting up, and the rain fell on frozen ground for three days. The water immediately ran off into the rivers—the Wabash, the Mississinewa, the White River, and others—and more than six hundred persons in Indiana and western Ohio were drowned in the resulting floods.

The character of Indiana industry changed fast after 1900, and the volume of manufacture rose rapidly Pork packing had been the largest and almost the only industry of real importance since 1845.

Coal deposits had been noted in the state in territorial days, but wood was so plentiful and cheap that real mining did not start until after the Civil War. Coal production in a dozen counties near the lower Wabash River increased from a million tons a year in 1880 to twenty-five million tons in 1920. Of relatively poor quality, the soft coal was used mostly for Indiana and Chicago industries and for heating purposes.

Hoosier pride was touched to the quick when John Gunther, in his *Inside U.S.A.*, called Indianapolis in the late 1940s the "dirtiest capital city" in America, alluding to the grime deposited on its buildings by the soft-coal smoke. Regular sand-blasting of public buildings, and conversion to other fuels have resulted in a different atmosphere today.

FOX HUNTING WAS POPULAR in rural areas of southern Indiana at the beginning of the century, a recreation brought by the first Anglo-Saxon settlers from Old Virginia and Maryland. (Hohenberger)

THE CHARM AND GRACE of an 1870 costume is modeled by this young Hoosier in the early 1900s. Unidentified, the setting of the photograph appears to be the Benjamin Harrison mansion in Indianapolis, and the gown probably that of Mrs. Harrison, the president's wife. (Lilly)

THE NEW WEST BADEN SPRINGS Hotel, shown here in the early 1900s, had 700 rooms and was built in 1902 to replace one destroyed by fire the year before. It was originally built in 1851 by John R. Lane, an itinerant medicine man exploiting the saline-sulphur waters there. Of unexampled elegance, the hotel, which included a huge gambling casino, advertised as "The Carlsbad of America." Going bankrupt in the Depression, it was later converted to a Jesuit College, and is now Northwood University. (ISL)

James Whitcomb Riley, who had become famous by 1900, inspired and encouraged other Hoosiers to take up the quill. The Bobbs-Merrill Publishing Company, organized at the turn of the century, promoted Indiana authors whose output increased significantly. Maurice Thompson and Booth Tarkington produced bestselling novels in 1899, and for the next fifty years Indiana writers dominated the American bestseller lists as did the residents of no other state. Several studies show Indiana either first or second by a slight margin to New York State, which has nearly three times the population.

Gene Stratton-Porter's books sold more than ten million copies in hardback—a record never equalled by any other American writer. Other Indiana authors of bestsellers during the five decades were Charles Major, Theodore Dreiser, Lloyd C. Douglas, Meredith Nicholson, John T. and George Barr McCutcheon, George Ade, Kin Hubbard, Albert Beveridge, Charles and Mary Beard, Mary Fellows Johnston, William Vaughn Moody, and Johnny Gruelle. Gruelle's *Raggedy Ann* and Major's *Bears of the Blue River* became immortal childhood classics, still popular today.

During the late 1800s, Indiana had grown in population and sophistication and acquired considerable political clout. It had contributed a president, Benjamin Harrison of Indianapolis, and five vice presidents, Schuyler Colfax, Thomas Hendricks, Charles W. Fairbanks, Thomas R. Marshall, and Levi Morton.

Among the state's powerful political figures was James (Jim) Watson, of Rushville, who spent thirty-five years in the House of Representatives and the U. S. Senate, long serving as the Republican whip, until 1933. Thomas Taggart, John W. Kern, Samuel R. Ralston, and Sen. Albert Beveridge, gained respect for Indiana's political machine on the national scene.

The Great Depression hit the state in the early thirties and changed Indiana life drastically. Some industrial cities were so strongly affected that from thirty to fifty percent of the population was on relief.

Indiana's politicians soon gained national headlines by unconventional methods. Being a "joiner" had always been a Hoosier characteristic. When the Ku Klux Klan was revived in the 1920s, the movement spread under Supreme Wizard Hiram Evans of Georgia into the North, especially to Indiana and Ohio. His organizer in Indiana was D. C. Stephenson, an ex-Texas printer, who became a superlative organizer and rabble-rouser.

When Evans, fearing his growing power, deposed him as dragon of the Indiana Klan, Stephenson successfully led a revolt and bolted from the United Klan. He built a new Indiana Klan organization more powerful than Evans had ever dreamed of. In the mid-1920s, it became virtually impossible to win public office in Indiana without Klan endorsement. Republican Ed Jackson, for instance, went into the governor's office under Klan auspices. Stephenson by the way, was reputed to have made several million dollars as his percentage of Klan-membership and -regalia income.

The Klan collapsed like a punctured balloon when Stephenson was convicted in 1925 of the sadistic rape-murder of Madge Overholtzer, an Indianapolis girl of respectable family. Gov. Ed Jackson had said when Stephenson was indicted that, if convicted, he would pardon the Klansman. When Stephenson received a life sentence, Jackson did not dare to do so.

In the 1932 election, Paul V. McNutt, distinguished-looking white-haired ex-commander of the American Legion, who caught the eye of state chairman R. Earl Peters as having political potential, won his first political office when he became Governor. He was swept into office on the Depression-born Roosevelt landslide. The overwhelmingly Democratic Assembly backed his reorganization of state government, and his administration was so efficient and successful that it almost approached being autocratic.

His successor, M. Clifford Townsend, of Hartford City and Marion won readily with a campaign enlivened by Townsend's coon-hunting stories. "Hoosier Homespun" came naturally to Townsend, a down-to-earth farmer and county school superintendent, and paid off at the polls. His successor was Henry F. Schricker, notable for his big white hat, the gregarious editor of a small-town weekly newspaper in Knox, Indiana, who had the same homespun qualities and the good common horse-sense of the rural Hoosier. He followed Schricker, learned to cope and cooperate with the Republican legislature and became one of the most popular governors the state ever had.

In 1940, Paul McNutt cast his eye on higher office. He almost came close to taking the Democratic National Nomination Convention that year by storm with a cleverly-organized plan that included packing the visitors' galleries with vociferous rooters. Pres. Franklin D. Roosevelt was so alarmed at the Hoosier upstart's move that McNutt, who had held several Federal posts, was banished to the Phillipines where he ended a meteoric career as governor-general.

Ingenuity and a homespun Hoosier image paid off in politics again when a virtual unknown, Wendell L. Willkie, started his political career at the absolute top—running for the presidency in 1940. In an unconventional campaign, run mostly by rank amateurs, he successfully stormed the G.O.P. convention. With rumpled suit and unruly hair, the native of Elwood, who maintained a home and seven farms in Rush County, became a popular hero. He broke F.D.R.'s firm grip on the electorate by gaining 22,000,000 votes even in defeat. His book, *One World*, published in 1943, was a surprising reversal of the isolationism and conservatism of Republican political leaders of the time. Willkie, who had been a Socialist while attending Indiana University, and a Democrat until 1936, provided an entirely new direction for his Republican followers.

The 1930s and 1940s were troubled times in Indiana. In addition to Depression and the Klan, the state was besieged by troubles brought on by crime,

ONE OF INDIANA'S worst train wrecks occurred in October 1903, when a Purdue University football special on the Monon Railroad collided with another train as it was entering Indianapolis. The twenty-six fatalities included most of the Purdue varsity players. One of the injured was Harry G. Leslie, who recovered to become governor of the state. The Purdue team was scheduled to play the first important college game ever scheduled in Indianapolis when the tragic wreck occurred inside the city. Rescuers and the curious thronged to the scene. (Purdue)

THIS WEST MAIN STREET barbershop in LaPorte had individual shaving mugs for its prized customers around 1904. Barbers shown are John LaFountain (owner), Harry Hardenbrook, and John A. Reiter. (LPHS)

FOOD PRESERVATION became big business in Indiana during the 1900s. Van Camp, at Indianapolis, had pioneered packing pork and beans as Civil War "K-rations." Hand-wrapping cans of the same product are these neat ladies at a H. J. Heinz plant. (Heinz)

FEW CORPORATION HEADS ever fraternized as much with their workers as did H. J. (57 Varieties) Heinz. Known as the "Prince of Paternalists," the 64-year-old Heinz is shown (on the wagon) speaking to pickle pickers in one of the company's contracted pickle fields near Walkerton, in 1907. (Heinz)

Prohibition, and racial friction, and the weather. The Ohio River cities suffered five hundred million dollars in damage during the floods of 1937, with heavy loss of life.

Wholesale layoffs in Indiana industries strengthened labor leaders who had abandoned socialism for the strong leadership provided by the AFL and the CIO. Union history was made when the United Automobile Workers went international at their convention in South Bend in 1936. During this convention, the CIO leadership successfully wooed UAW members in separate meetings and influenced enough of them to swing their affiliation from the AFL to the CIO. In the process, UAW president Homer Martin, a minister from Kansas City, was ousted. Martin and the press subsequently charged that the new leadership was dominated by Communists, whose newspaper, *The Daily Worker*, was lying about in big stacks.

The new unionism made rapid strides in most industrial cities of the state. A new strike technique was introduced shortly thereafter when the UAW called for the first sit-down strike against the Bendix auto parts plant in South Bend.

On the right wing of politics, the jailed Klansman Stephenson was replaced by such demagogues as William Dudley Pelley, Gerald L. K. Smith, and Court Asher. All of them had only a fraction of Stephenson's following.

Pelley, a gifted New England newspaperman and magazine fiction writer, had a penchant for trouble. He moved his printing business to Indianapolis when North Carolina state authorities wanted him for illegal sale of securities, and promoted there a new religion that he had founded along with his Nazi Silver Shirts. After the Silver Shirts went underground, he was able to avoid jail both on charges by the Department of Justice as well as the Internal Revenue Service. The government did finally send him to prison on sedition charges during World War II because of his writings opposing the war.

Gerald L. K. Smith, a Protestant minister in then-suburban Indianapolis, liked to lambast minority groups just like Pelley. He was at one time a close associate of the dictatorial governor of Louisiana, Huey Long, and later also of the fiery reactionary priest in Detroit, Father Charles Edward Coughlin.

Both the Depression and Prohibition contributed to Indiana's most flamboyant era of crime. St. Louis mobsters moved into the state. With headquarters at Terre Haute, they were reported to have forced nearby farmers into setting up a network of moonshine stills in the area. Others in the Southern Indiana hills and elsewhere went into moonshining on their own volition. Fast cars, with hired guns accompanying the drivers, ran bootleg liquor from Chicago into Indianapolis to ease parched throats.

Small-town desperadoes, with pistols and fast cars, emulated Jesse James in the myth of "robbing the rich and giving to the poor," the rich being the

GARY became a modern miracle after 1906 when U. S. Steel started construction of a plant, a harbor, and a city on a desolate track of barren sand and sloughs. By 1940, it had over 100,000 population. The upper view shows construction of the slip and turning basin for the harbor, in 1907 or 1908. Below, workmen line the dock to hear speeches by company and city officials from the deck of a great newly-arrived Great Lakes ore carrier. Below, Judge Elbert H. Gary, president of U. S. Steel, for whom the city was named. Many other steel, oil, cement, and other industrial giants later located their plants in the adjacent Lake Michigan corridor. (USS)

banks and the poor being the gunmen and their associates. These Hoosiers had capable predecessors, particularly in the notorious Reno gang of Jackson County, who originated the quaint and colorful custom of train robbery at Seymour in 1866.

The Dillinger gang, the Brady gang, and lone-handed Gene Alger were popular heroes of many, and a terror to banks and lawmen in the early 1930s. Lurid national headlines heralded their exploits. John Dillinger passed into a legend that will long endure by bold holdups, brazen robberies of police station arsenals, jail breaks, and manhunts. He was mowed down in an F.B.I. ambush at a Chicago theatre on July 22, 1934.

The Brady gang also gained notoriety with a similar but shorter career, including a spectacular jail break. The gang was wiped out with the exception of James Dahlhover, when police were alerted and ambushed the gang in a Maine store holdup, far from their native Indiana. Gene Alger was less adept and luckier. A Butler University student, whose professors thought he had a great future as a poet, Alger's only confederate was his girl friend, the daughter of a New Albany sheriff. Robbing banks to pay college expenses and buy gifts for his girl, Alger was soon caught and sent to prison.

Surely, Indiana never knew more excitement and turmoil in peacetime than in the 1930s. Mayor Jack Edwards, of Marion, one of the state's most headline-conscious politicians, even bought an armored car to protect himself and other City Fathers from bandits.

The Thirties brought some profound changes in the rural areas. Most farmers barely made expenses, as overproduction brought ruinously low prices, and many of them living on the poorer land in hilly areas of Southern Indiana were not even able to pay taxes. Their land was repossessed, and much of it converted into state and national forests.

When World War II broke out, neither Indiana nor the nation realized that this war would be the biggest and costliest in history, and that the world, subjected to profound changes, would never be the same again.

When the United States entered the war, Hoosiers were drafted or enlisted in large numbers. Fort Benjamin Harrison at Indianapolis was soon filled to capacity with recruits, and Camp Atterbury near Columbus was established for their training.

Industries whose assembly lines had been working at less than capacity soon were geared up for new activities, though they were unaccustomed to the new products, and manpower was extremely short. Allison in Indianapolis produced airplane engines, Studebaker trucks and tanks; International Harvester in Fort Wayne switched to trucks; Anaconda provided copper wires and cables; Howard's in New Albany manufactured naval landing craft; a giant naval ordnance plant opened near Shoals; a powder plant at Charlestown; and an Air Force Base at Bunker Hill.

A PIONEER INDIANA AVIATOR was Arthur Ray Smith, the Fort Wayne barnstormer who was known as the "Boy Wizard of the Sky." His boyish mind was inflamed by the feats of fellow Hoosiers Orville and Wilbur Wright, who made their first successful plane flight at Kitty Hawk in December 1903, and he decided to become a flyer. In 1906, then sixteen, he talked his parents into mortgaging their house so that he could build his own plane. It did fly—to New Haven, about ten miles away. Smith was in business as a barnstormer. He was one of the flying daredevils at the Panama-Pacific Exposition in 1915, and one of a group of American barnstormers who took their planes to Japan in 1916, the first ever to fly in that country. He died in a crash while carrying the airmail in 1926. (FWPL)

[120]

ROBINSON PARK in Fort Wayne spelled romantic recreation for the young women of the town. There they could venture onto an artificial lake in a rented boat, a gallant male providing insurance against a nautical disaster and an awning assuring that the sun would not spoil their fashionable lily-white complexions. Leg-of-mutton sleeves and sailor hats had come into style. (FWHS)

Hoosier farmers were short on manpower, too, but they produced more food than ever before despite scarcity of fuel, fertilizer, and other supplies. More food than ever was shipped overseas, not only for American forces, but also for their allies.

Within a year or so, civilians felt many shortages, particularly in tires, gasoline, cigarettes, and food. Rationing began. Hoosier civilians tightened their belts, but there was little actual suffering. With nearly full employment and high wages, people were able to buy the necessities, and forwent their accustomed luxuries with little grumbling.

As the war effort geared up, Hoosiers moved as never before. Many went elsewhere in the state or to shipyards or plane factories on the coasts, and the demand for workers surged, in addition to those entering the service. "Rosie the Riveter" became a national heroine. In Indiana, girls and women who had worked for peanuts during the Depression as clerks, secretaries, dime store clerks, and waitresses, soon converted to highly-paid production line workers, filling the majority of jobs heretofore held by men. Hoosiers, considered "isolationists," who had very strongly supported Sen. Robert Taft of Ohio, soon were aware this was a different kind of a war. It was global in extent; it was immense in casualties, and in armament of tanks and aircraft and atomic weapons.

Word of terrible naval battles in the Pacific, of allied defeats on land and in the air, brought the peril of the situation home. And then came the news of loved ones killed and wounded in foreign countries.

When everything looked the gloomiest, the Russians repelled the Nazi drive at Stalingrad. The Battle of Midway in the Pacific on June 4, 1942, gave America hope that the mighty victory surge of the Japanese could be halted. Then came D-Day on June 6, 1944. The years 1944 and 1945 meant more production and more belt-tightening, but the future looked far brighter. Victory arrived with V-E Day on May 8, 1945, followed by Hiroshima and then V-J Day in September.

Indiana soon was on the way to something resembling normalcy as factories reconverted to take care of the great pent-up demand for new cars, tires and civilian goods of all kinds. But normal life had hardly been reestablished when a new conflict, the Korean War, broke out. Technical advances, industrial building, the hurly-burly of the war years, and the mobility habits developed by 1950 gave an entirely different aspect to Indiana. While the homespun Hoosier image remains, its likeness can only be glimpsed today in remote, small rural towns. Even there, the farmer may still go to town on errands in blue jeans, but on Sunday and on vacation only the practiced can tell him from the city dweller. And his net worth is likely to be greater, as his farmstead is entirely mechanized and electrified, and his average investment of $100,000 to 500,000 would be enough to build and equip a small factory.

By the end of the decade, the character of Indiana's industries had changed entirely. The resourceful young Hoosier farmer, mechanic, or blacksmith who developed a better product and a new industry (like Studebaker, Oliver, Singer, Allison, or Howard) apparently turned his energies to politics.

From 1940 to 1950, Indiana had some of the most powerful and influential political leaders in Wendell L. Willkie; Ernest M. Morris of South Bend, the G.O.P. national chairman; Paul S. Hoffman, an ex-Studebaker president who headed the Marshall Plan in Europe; Frank E. McKinney of Indianapolis, the national Democratic Party chairman under President Truman; U. S. Senators Homer Capehart and William E. Jenner; Republican whip Charles W. Halleck; and war-time governors Henry Schricker and Ralph W. Gates.

Virtually none of the industrial giants were headquartered in the state. Studebaker, the lone auto-maker, was still struggling for survival in 1950, before it gave up auto-making and moved to Canada. National Homes in Lafayette, a manufacturer of prefabricated homes, and Central Soya of Decatur, a soybean processor, grew with leaps and bounds and, while not among "Fortune's One Hundred," were almost alone among Indiana-based enterprises. Cities throughout the state did have large factories now, but they were only branches of the big automobile companies, the giant oil corporations, and others.

Most of the crossroads-general stores and "Pop and Mom" groceries had perished in the 1930s. An ill-conceived state gross income tax schedule had accomplished quickly what was probably inevitable, in any event. A few rugged individualists are holding out, mostly in the smaller towns, but the giant merchandising chains now get most of the Hoosier's dollar. The state's newspapers are the lone exception to this trend. Six Indiana dailies, at Indianapolis and elsewhere, controlled by the Pulliams, as well as several other important papers, are holdouts against the national trend to chain operation.

Contact with and awareness of the rest of the world in World War II even has changed Hoosier voting patterns as well as the state's complexion. Conservative extremists since World War II have been limited mostly to the small number of members of the John Birch Society which was formed at a meeting with Robert Welch in an Indianapolis home in 1958.

Old-time Hoosiers sometimes are amazed when looking at the mores, customs, and way of life today. Few of the young generation are even vaguely aware of what it is to split firewood; to clean the kerosene lamp and trim the wick; to curry a horse and harness him to a carriage; to put up ice or make apple butter; to pare potatoes or dress a chicken; to ride an interurban or the railroad cars behind a steam engine; to drain the crankcase and the car's radiator for the winter; or to attend the affectionately-remembered little red one-room school. They are only part of nostalgic Hoosier memories now!

INDIANAPOLIS IN 1901—This excellent view of downtown Indianapolis, facing west, was taken from the top of the Soldiers and Sailors Monument to show the smoke from an industrial blaze at the rear of the Statehouse, which occupies the center. The hazy background is due to coal smoke belching from factory stacks. The soot from this soft coal caused John Gunther three decades later to call Indianapolis the "dirtiest capital city in the United States" in his book *Inside U. S. A.* Resentful Hoosiers took the remark to heart, adopted fuel regulations, and regularly sandblasted public buildings to prove Gunther wrong. (ISL)

[123]

EVERY CITY HAD a first-class hotel in the old days, and in Indianapolis it was the Claypool at Illinois and Washington in the first five decades of the twentieth century. Numerous local and national celebrities used it as a gathering place for elegant banquets and important conventions, political and otherwise. It took over the prestige held earlier by the Bates House. The grand hotel (shown in 1907) fell upon evil days along with many others in the 1960s, suffering a disastrous fire. It has recently been razed. (ISL)

A TRAFFIC JAM occurred one block away from the "Crossroads of America," at Illinois and Washington (northeast corner) in 1904. Electric streetcars had largely supplanted the horse-drawn ones, but the new-fangled automobile had not replaced wagons and buggies. It was "every man for himself" at crossings, and pedestrians had a perilous way to go. (ISL)

SIDEWALK SUPERINTENDENTS got a thrill as they watched this women's group prepare to take off on a tour in the new Indianapolis sight-seeing bus in May 1907. The building at left rear appears to be the Board of Trade Building, still standing. (ISL)

SCHOOL CHILDREN in Indiana walked to the little red schoolhouse, or were taken by their parents until about 1908. Then the Fall Creek Township school of Marion County engaged the first "kid hack." With horses pulling and pupils pushing, the high-wheeled hack could navigate snowdrifts and mudholes that no motorist would dare to try . (ISL)

MEN WILL RACE, and surely the zaniest auto race of all times was one which crossed Indiana in 1908. It probably inflamed the nimble minds of Carl Fisher and other Hoosier and Midwest racers who would make Indiana a world racing center within a few years. Several nations were represented in the crews of six cars which, racing for a $25,000 prize, started in New York on February 12. The first cars had crossed the United States only four years before; many areas had no roads whatever, and the drivers drove to Valdez, Alaska through the Western Canadian Rockies, planning to drive across Bering Strait on the ice, and then cross trackless Siberian wilderness and mountains. The strait could not be crossed; they backtracked to Seattle, transported the cars by ship to Vladivostok, and continued. Virtually no one thought they could cross the United States in the dead of winter, but they did. Three actually reached Paris, led by the American entry, the Thomas Flyer, driven by Montague Roberts and George Schuster (*top*) which arrived July 30. The Italian Zust, with crew, (*center*) looks more like a polar expedition. The French de Dion (*bottom*) with a real Arctic explorer, Capt. Hans Hensen, in its crew, had to withdraw at Vladivostok. Northern Indiana's unpaved dirt roads provided much digging and pushing as an exceptional late winter thaw turned the roads into a major obstacle in the form of gumbo mud. The route across the state led to Chicago, via Furnessville.

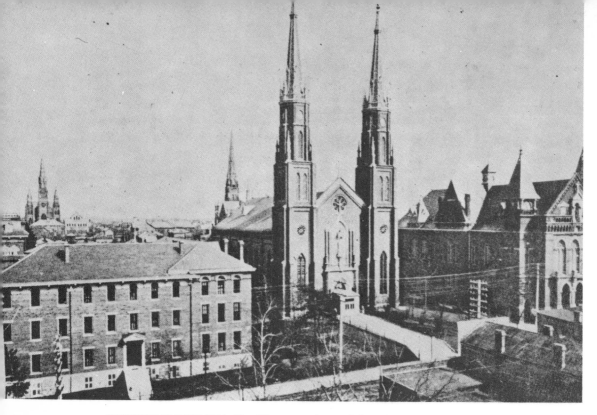

CATHEDRAL SQUARE in Fort Wayne, southeast of the main business district, as it looked sixty years ago: From left to right are St. Augustine's Academy, the Cathedral, and Library Hall (later Central Catholic High School). (FWPL)

FORT WAYNE'S WORST FIRE occurred on May 3, 1908, when the historic Aveline Hotel, the leading hostelry of the city for more than four decades, caught fire. The five-story structure at the southeast corner of Berry and Calhoun streets was built at the beginning of the Civil War by Francis S. Aveline, a prominent citizen of French blood, who came to the city in 1820. Twelve roomers died in the blaze. (FWPL)

THE FORT WAYNE POLICE FORCE on parade about 1910: Over the center of the street is the sign of Wolf & Dessauer, the city's leading department store until well after World War II, now out of business. (FWHS)

MANY HOOSIER YOUTHS did Army service in an almost forgotten U. S. campaign, the Filipino Insurrection led by Aguinaldo. These three members of the occupation army in the Philippines, after the revolt was quelled, were photographed in 1909. Charles Dudley of Sullivan is at the lower left. (Wilcox)

THE FIVE WATKINS BROTHERS of Kosciusko County all served in the Union Union Army during the Civil War and lived into the twentieth century. John is second from right; other names not available.

[127]

FRANK McKINNEY HUBBARD
created "Abe Martin of Brown County,"
a rustic cartoon character whose sayings
in Hoosier dialect first appeared in 1904
in the *Indianapolis News*. Hubbard's
homespun Hoosier wit and humor
seventy years later are still reprinted
daily in several of the largest American
dailies, and are enshrined among com-
pilations of epigrams of all time.
(Pulliam)

JOHN T. MCCUTCHEON, son of a Tippecanoe County livestock trader, based many
of his famous cartoons in the *Chicago Tribune* and *Chicago Record-Herald* on his
native Indiana. In this scene, published
about 1904, he makes fun of the already
well-known tendency of Hoosiers to write.
Among famous authors of the day were his
brother, George Barr McCutcheon, author of
Graustark and many other successful mystery novels. His cartoon, "Indiana Summer,"
has become a traditional classic, having been
reprinted each October for more than five
decades on the front page of the *Chicago
Tribune*.

INDIANA AUTHORS WERE dominant
figures in literary circles throughout the
first five decades of the 1900s. Four of
them, all authors of best-sellers, posed
together for this celebrated photograph
about 1910. They are James Whitcomb
Riley and Meredith Nicholson, at rear,
and George Ade and Booth Tarkington,
foreground. (News)

THEODORE E. DREISER, who was brought up in Indiana, is seldom mentioned as a Hoosier author, although several of his books are based on his childhood in Terre Haute, Sullivan, and Kosciusko County. His only college education was one year at Indiana University. Controversial and avant-garde later, he is pictured about 1908 when he was editing *Delineator*, a namby-pamby magazine for women. (VCHS)

GENE STRATTON-PORTER, shown in gardening costume, with trowel, at her rustic cottage at Lake Geneva, never received the literary praise of other Indiana authors. She nevertheless is probably the most-beloved of all today. Her novels, starting with the *Song of the Cardinal* in 1903, have sold more than ten million hardback copies—a record unequalled by any other American author. They featured idyllic romances in rural settings and did much to foster interest in natural history and ecology. (ISL)

[129]

JAMES WHITCOMB RILEY was known as the Children's Poet, and his home on Lockerbie Street in Indianapolis was the scene of many pilgrimages by admiring Hoosier school children. David Randall, the head of the Lilly Library, estimates that Riley earned two million dollars from sale of his poetry, a record surely not approached by any other American poet. (ISL)

FEW EVER SAW SUCH CHANGES in Indiana as Kilsoquah, granddaughter of the great Miami chief, Little Turtle, shown on her hundredth birthday at Roanoke in 1910. The man is her part-French son, Anthony Revarre. (FWHS)

VIRTUAL WASTE LAND was most of the Calumet region of northwestern Indiana in 1900. Adjacent to Chicago, it was to burst into importance as one of the world's greatest industrial areas in the next three decades. The photo at left shows Standard Oil Company of Indiana's first installation alongside the Hammond and Indiana railroad track about 1900. The lower view shows the immense Whiting refinery of the corporation in 1910. (Standard)

AUTOMOBILES were fancied up with many accessories by the time these gents about 1910 were ready to start a hunting trip by car. Note the dashboard, with tool box mounted on it, doors for the rear tonneau, folding top, rubber bulb horn, and carbide lights—and, we mustn't forget, fenders to catch the mud.

A BRAVE HOOSIER was Rose E. Melville of Indianapolis who drove her own sporty Pope-Hartford car. The photo was taken in front of a downtown garage on February 20, 1906. (ISL)

[131]

PARKING FOR AUTOS had replaced the hitchrack on Ohio Street, facing the present post office, when the photo was taken previous to World War I. The large building is the Hume-Mansur Building, long a center for doctors' offices. Note the variety of designs, all with high wheels to negotiate muddy and rutted dirt roads. (ISL)

CARL FISHER, founder of the Indianapolis Motor Speedway inspects initial construction work at the Indianapolis Motor Speedway track, at Speedway City, in 1909. (Speedway)

CAPT. EDDIE RICKENBACKER was a popular Indianapolis racer before he became the renowned World-War-I aviation ace. Here he is at the wheel of his Indianapolis-made Duesenberg in 1914. Rickenbacker bought the Indianapolis Motor Speedway in 1927 after Fisher, then developing Miami Beach, lost interest. He added a golf course to the property in 1929. (Speedway)

[132]

START OF THE FIRST 500-mile race at the Indianapolis Motor Speedway in 1911. Ray Harroun averaged 74.59 m.p.h., to lead the forty entries competing for $25,000 in prizes to victory. He drove a Hoosier-made 6-cylinder Marmon Wasp. (Speedway)

INDIANA AND WESTERN OHIO were hit by one of the nation's most terrible floods in 1913. More than six hundred lives were lost, survivors suffered intensely from cold and exposure, and damage ran into the hundreds of millions of dollars. Peru was engulfed by the waters of the Wabash and Mississinewa river which converge above it, and suffered the worst destruction and loss of life of any Indiana city. Beginning on March 24, 1913, the rain fell for four days without letting up, melting the snow on the ground which swelled the flooded streams even more. When the floods subsided, the picture was grim *(top)*. At the peak of the flood, only two small islands of land remained in Peru. Many people were rescued from the roofs of their houses by boat or, in shallower waters, by mule-drawn wagon *(center)*, and taken to the Courthouse where food brought in by the Coast Guard was distributed. The rampaging White River also left only kindling wood in its wake, witnessed by this train and railroad bridge *(below)* in Indianapolis. The capital suffered very heavy damage, but little loss of life. (ISL-Bone)

BROWN COUNTY CARRIAGES await the coming of the train at the tiny hamlet of Helmsburg about 1910. It was the only railway station in the county, and the principal outlet to the outside world at the time. The Nashville hack (horse-drawn) heads the line. (Lilly)

BROWN COUNTY BOYS, caught skinnydipping in "the ole swimmin' hole" about 1915, are sitting on a rocky ledge below the pool, probably Beanblossom Creek or Salt Creek, not the "Old Brandywine" of Riley's poem, which is in nearby Hancock County. (Lilly)

RARELY SEEN TODAY, the farm draft horse provided power for many Hoosier farmers well into the twentieth century. This three-horse hitch is plowing with its owner, Orville Clem of Cass County, at the reins.

NORTHERN INDIANA BECAME an important dairying area in the twentieth century, providing milk not only for its own cities but such metropolises as Chicago. This view is of the Brookside Dairy Farm, owned by John H. Bass in Allen County, as it appeared in 1913. Two windmills, pumping water for the Holstein cows without fuel cost, anticipated the energy crisis. (FWPL)

[135]

PRIOR TO 1916, there were virtually no paved highways of any kind in Indiana. Automobiles, whose numbers were fast increasing, made their way the best they could over unsurfaced dirt and a few gravel roads. Most cars were put in the barn for the winter and when they ventured out in warm weather, the thawed roads were often quagmires as this one somewhere in rural Indiana.

HORSE AND SLIP SCOOP were the standard road-making equipment in the first decade of the 1900s in Indiana.

INDIANA STATE HIGHWAY employee Tom Goby is shown beside the commission's Model-T Ford in the 1920s, parked in the "ford" of a southern Indiana stream. Most of the streams on back roads of the area were unbridged then, but federal matching of highway funds had brought the start of a modern highway system in the state.

THIS UNIDENTIFIED STERNWHEELER being greeted in 1915 by a well-dressed crowd on the Indiana shore of the Ohio appears to be an excursion boat. (ISL)

BROAD RIPPLE AMUSEMENT PARK, then beyond the city limits on White River, was perhaps the busiest recreational facility during World War I days. Riverside Park also was popular. (ISL)

THOMAS RILEY MARSHALL, of North Manchester and Columbia City, was vice president under Woodrow Wilson when World War I broke out. He served a record two terms. He is probably best remembered for his witty observation that "what this country needs is a good five-cent cigar." But it was first said by Kin Hubbard's "Abe Martin." Other Kin Hubbard epigrams have been credited to Mark Twain. (Adams)

[138]

PATRIOTISM had double meaning when Fort Wayne celebrated the Indiana State Centennial in 1916. World War I had started; the parade assumed martial aspects, and "Old Glory" was much in evidence. (FWPL)

INTERNATIONAL HARVESTER Company, whose
truck manufacturing plant is at Fort Wayne, made a
reputation when its new low-wheeled truck became
the first to scale Pike's Peak in Colorado in 1916.
This 1917 model, which has the radiator behind the
engine, was manufactured by the thousands for the
U. S. Army in World War I.

A WORLD WAR I RALLY, preceded by a parade, was held in downtown Lawrenceburg in 1917 or
1918. Parade floats, not yet today's elaborate elegant affairs, depended mainly on draping now-anti-
quated cars with red-white-and-blue bunting and crepe paper. At the rear of the crowd are two smaller
figures clad in knickerbockers, a common badge of schoolboys. (ISL)

[139]

FORT BENJAMIN HARRISON, just outside Indianapolis, became one of the nation's principal training camps for doughboys, as the infantry were called. The upper photo shows the huge tents which served as "barracks." In the center, two trainees spar in bayonet practice, of much use later in trench and man-to-man warfare overseas. The lower views show trench warfare practice. (Wilcox)

WOMEN FIRST WORKED in numbers in Indiana industries as young men went into the Army. These husky corn-fed Hoosier belles replaced men at the Whiting Refinery of Standard Oil Company (Indiana) in 1918. They seem pleased as punch that the company photographer was preserving a record of their patriotic efforts. (Standard)

THESE FOUR ARTISTS of the Hoosier school were undoubtedly prominent but are not identified. They donated their talents to painting a victory mural on a building near Meridian and Ohio streets in Indianapolis, to celebrate the armistice on November 11, 1918. (ISL)

[141]

PATRIOTIC HOOSIERS thronged downtown Indianapolis to celebrate the armistice and end of World War I on November 11, 1918. This scene is at the corner of Meridian and Ohio, looking north on Meridian. The four figures at lower right are the fine artists of the preceding photo. The sign, "To Hell with the Kaiser," was with the compliments of some employees of Link Belt, a very old Indianapolis industry which specialized in conveyors and was much involved in the war effort. (ISL)

INDIANA TURNED OUT with special hospitality in 1919 when, after armistice terms were signed, a company of "poilus" from the tiny nation of Belgium, which the Germans quickly overran as the war started, visited the city. They stand on the steps in Monument Circle, with the sturdy "war dogs" who pulled supplies in carts. (ISL)

ONE OF THE GREATEST WELCOMES ever afforded a visiting dignitary was given Marshal Ferdinand Foch, who visited Indianapolis on November 4, 1921. Hoosiers recognized him as the man who had guided the Allies to a quick victory over the Entente Powers while supreme commander of all Allied Forces in France. Culver Military Academy's famed "Black Horse Troop" is shown circling the Soldiers and Sailors Monument. (ISL)

A BYZANTINE-ARCHITECTURE VOGUE
gripped Indiana as elsewhere about 1900. The Ala-
hambra Theater on Washington near Illinois Street
is shown as it was in 1916. Legitimate theatre,
vaudeville, and movies all used its stage and screen.
(ISL)

THE KNIGHTS OF PYTHIAS BUILDING (shown
in 1915) at Massachusetts and Pennsylvania was
long an Indianapolis landmark. It was demolished
about 1968 to make room for the Indiana National
Bank Building. (ISL)

INDIANA CIVILIANS suffered severely during World War I. Thousands died from the influenza epidemic of 1918-1919 and the intense cold of the winter of 1917-1918. On one of the rare occasions in which the Ohio River froze over, the *City of Louisville,* a long familiar visitor at Indiana river ports, was crushed in the ice at Cincinnati and sank.

INTENSE COLD gripped northern Indiana, with far-below zero temperatures and impassable snow-drifts, in the winter of 1917-1918. The sap in giant trees froze to the center, causing them to explode with cannon-like reports. This view shows the pier and lighthouse in Michigan City, beloved beacons of summer tourists. (LPHS)

PERU BECAME THE CAPITAL of the American circus world in the early 1900s, thanks to Ben Wallace, local owner of a circus, who in 1907 bought the Wild Animal Show of Carl Hagenbeck of Hamburg, Germany, the world's greatest wild-animal importer and dealer. Wallace quartered it nearby on his large farm in the Mississinewa River valley. He later sold to Mugivan and Bowers' American Circus Corporation, which also quartered such famous shows as Al G. Barnes, John Robinson, Yankee Robinson, Sells Floto and Sparks Circus—all advertising as "the World's Largest." Mugivan and Bowers sold out to Ringling Brothers in 1930, as the Great Depression hit the circus business. These are Hagenbeck-Wallace elephants rehearsing at the farm in 1929.

[145]

WALLACE & HAGENBECK'S CIRCUS held a gala dress rehearsal, outdoors, at its Peru headquarters each spring before going on the road by train. The farm manager's home is at rear of the performing elephants, pictured in 1929, and the building at right was used to house animals in winter. The farm was later bought by Emil Schram, retired president of the New York Stock Exchange and a native of Peru.

EMMETT KELLEY, the best-known and most-beloved circus clown, was one of many famous performers who called the Wallace farm at Peru "home" after the season ended for the tent shows in the 1920s. (ISL)

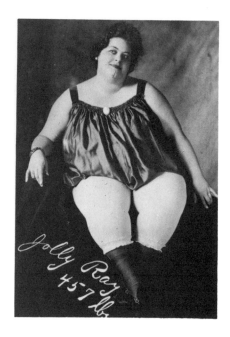

EVERY CIRCUS SIDESHOW had its "fat lady." This is Jolly Ray, weight 457 pounds, according to the caption on the photo. This kind of hyperbole and exaggeration, of course, went hand-in-hand with circuses, ever since Barnum remarked that "there's a sucker born every minute." (ISL)

GRANDDADDY OF MODERN CIRCUSES, the P. T. Barnum Circus was organized in 1871, and eventually became Barnum & Bailey's. It was a frequent visitor to Indiana, and a dreaded competitor of the Indiana-based shows. This poster depicted its splendors in the early 1900s. (ISL)

THE "GIRLIE" SHOW was a standard part of circus sideshows. The abbreviated skirts of these synthetic Oriental harem beauties were considered quite daring and risque by Hoosier women just prior to 1920. Before the end of the next decade, young "flappers" would be wearing them shorter. (ISL)

"FOREIGN" BEAUTIES, in skimpy and exotic costumes, were standard attractions of circus parades and performances in the great days of the train shows. Oh, my goodness, did you see the lighted cigarette in the hand of the girl to the right—a scandalous thing indeed for a woman in those days. (ISL)

SCARCELY ANY HAMLET in Indiana went without some kind of live entertainment in the early 1900s, either in the form of "Uncle Tom's Cabin" tent shows or dog-and-pony-shows, until the Great Depression. This is the "menagerie" of the Eiler show. Gentry Bros. Dog and Pony, with headquarters at Bloomington, Indiana, was one of the leaders in this field from 1885 to 1934, at times having several units playing different places, all under the Gentry name. (ISL)

[147]

NASHVILLE, the Brown County Seat, is portrayed about 1924 by Minturn, the wood-block artist. He and others had already discovered the county's charms and maintained a cooperative gallery in the building in left foreground. Note the Melodeon Hall at right. (Lilly)

FRANK HOHENBERGER, artist with a camera, was an *Indianapolis Sun* printer who became a shutterbug. So bitten was he that he quit his job and retired to Nashville, the county seat of the rustic island of Brown County. Together with Kin Hubbard and Richard Lieber, he made the isolated area's rugged beauty and quaint charm known to the world. Today, thousands throng there each weekend, seeking relief from the jostling and the frustrations of city life. (Lilly)

ANTIQUE CAR BUFFS might offer sums of five or six figures for this handcranked Model-T fire truck, complete with equipment, proudly demonstrated here in the 1920s by the Nashville fire chief. (Hohenberger)

BROWN COUNTY FARMERS kept their horses long after others had adopted tractors. Small tillable acreages and the rugged terrain as well as the cost discouraged use of early tractors. (Lilly)

FINE THOROUGHBRED HORSE-flesh was as much prized in southern Indiana as Kentucky. This equine expert somewhere south of Indianapolis about 1920 is ascertaining the true measurement, in hands, not inches, at the horse's withers. (Lilly)

THIS BROWN COUNTIAN found the sure-footed donkeys well-adapted to the steep and rocky hills of his farm. The pole at the rear of the wagon operated primitive brakes which slowed the wagon going down hill, so that it would not run over the donkeys. (Lilly)

LOG CABINS, still commonly used as homes of the county's natives, were purchased by city residents joining the back-to-nature movements in the late 1920s and early 1930s in Brown County. The trackless snow indicates this one has been closed for the winter. (Hohenberger)

THE BROWN COUNTY SHERIFF (name unknown) was hardy but crime infrequent, so he had time to pose on the famous "Liar's Bench' following a snowfall at Nashville. The "Liar's Bench," where the men used to socialize after coming to town to shop or pay their taxes, is a tourist attraction today. (Hohenberger)

MOST INDIANA COUNTIES had school buses in the twenties, but these Brown County children still had to walk home, taking a shortcut across a snow-covered field. (Lilly)

THE SLEIGH and sled were common in the
1800s, but had become rare here in the 1920s.
This Southern Indiana farmer found the old bob-
sled still handy when he wanted to deliver a load
of corn fodder in town. (Hohenberger)

RENDERING LARD from the trimmings off
choice pork cuts was an important part of home
butchering, and required constant attention to
see that the melted fat did not scorch. Brown
county about 1920. (Lilly)

A BROWN COUNTY WOMAN and her children
get in the family wood supply with the aid of a
crosscut saw. Photographer Hohenberger had
much difficulty in photographing the native people of the county because they feared he was
"putting the evil eye" on them. (Lilly)

BROWN COUNTY FARMERS tilled the soil of the creek bottoms, leaving the craggy sandstone hills in forests, when this picture was taken in the 1920s. They were able to survive economically until ruinously low Depression prices left most of them unable to pay their taxes. Much of their land was

taken over by the state for forest preserves and for Brown County State Park, which is largest of all. (Hohenberger)

THE FARM THRESHING RING was a farm community institution in which neighbors worked shoulder-to-shoulder in the hot, sweaty job of threshing their wheat and oat crops in late summer. Farm women vied in providing bountiful "threshing dinners," which have no comparison today, for the hungry workers at noon. College students who wear bib overalls today may not realize these were standard uniforms and the badge of honest toil for Grant County farmers in the 1920s.

THE ROUND BARN was an invention calculated to eliminate haymow corners where it was difficult to store hay. Construction difficulties kept them few, and today they are landmarks for the curious. This one, located on a Marshall County farm, probably was built in the late 1800s.

MULTIPLE HORSE HITCHES were not confined to brewery wagons in the 1920s. Enterprising farmers, like this one in Cass County, devised either tandem or abreast gear in order to compete with the new-fangled tractors on difficult jobs requiring much power, such as disking cornstalks.

IS IT SMILE OR BLUSH this young woman is exhibiting? Her swimming costume donned for a vacation at a northern Indiana lake about 1920 would have been too daring for most older women of the time.

ORPHAN GIRLS LEARNED useful home crafts at the Brightside Home in Plymouth during the 1920s. The sewing machine in foreground is, of course, a Singer made at nearby South Bend. (ISL)

THE OLD PIONEER HANDICRAFTS, slightly modernized, were carried over into the twentieth century by a rug factory in Jennings County. This county was the scene of considerable excitement in 1863 when the Home Guard drew up to protect the courthouse at Vernon and bluffed the raider, Gen. John H. Morgan, out of his plan to capture the town and loot the county treasury. (ISL)

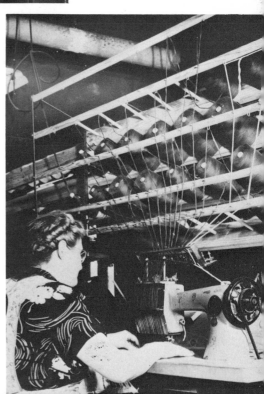

EQUINE POWER GAVE GROUND grudgingly before the new machines. This mule car was stll operating in 1927 on the Massachusetts-and-College-Avenue line in Indianapolis. (ISL)

THE DAYS OF STEAM still lingered on in the twenties. This traction engine (a steam engine on wheels) pulls a gargantuan load of crushed stone for a road-construction job at LaPorte. The steam tractor was probably an Advance-Rumley made locally. A roller has been substituted for the front wheels. (LPHS)

THE INDIANA SAND DUNES and adjoining Lake Michigan beaches are one of the nation's great scenic and recreational areas, which became the center of one of the first "Save-the-Ecology" movements in the early 1920s. When Congress failed to enact legislation to make the unique area a national park, Hoosiers, aided by philanthropists Elbert Gary and Julius Rosenwald, bought 2,200 acres with 3½ miles along Lake Michigan for the Indiana Dunes State Park. In 1972, the federal government finally dedicated an adjoining 10 miles of Lake Michigan shoreline as Indiana Dunes National Lakeshore, the first federal urban park. (Long)

"DIANA OF THE DUNES:" Alice Mabel Gray of Chicago, daughter of a physician, was fifty years ahead of her time. Well-educated, doing secretarial work for the University of Chicago, she got fed up with the big-city rat-race in 1915, and, cashing her last weekly pay check, walked away from it all to become a "lady hermit" in the wild Indiana sand-dune region of Lake County. Living in a shack, she was happy in her solitude, communing with nature, paying no rent, and living, at very little cost, the life of Thoreau. She might have lived happily and died unremembered, had she taken a bathing suit. But she was caught skinny-dipping on a remote Lake Michigan beach. Chicago and Calumet newspaper reporters hounded her incessantly, having found such an unconventional and sensational subject. She was usually uncommunicative, if they could locate her, and so more fiction than fact was published about the "Diana of the Dunes," as she was dubbed. Real tragedy entered her later life when she died of uremic poisoning in 1925 and was buried in Gary. "Diana" received probably far more space in Chicago newspapers than Mrs. Potter Palmer, the city's leading socialite. (G P-T)

[157]

MAIN STREET in Evansville in the early 1920s: The Intermediate Life Building is at left of the intersection. (EVC)

PRINCIPALS relax during a recess in the Speer case, a famous Dubois County case tried in Federal Court at Evansville in 1921. Main Street is in the background. (EVC)

THE TOWN OF WINONA LAKE, a quiet resort community on a pretty lake in Kosciusko County, is unique among Midwest towns. Entirely devoted to Protestant religious activities, its principal landmark is the Billy Sunday Tabernacle, named for the greatest evangelist of them all, William Ashley (Billy) Sunday. A reformed big-league baseball player, he arrived in 1895 with his wife Nellie (Ma) Sunday, became a Presbyterian minister, and is said to have preached to more than 100,000,000 people (before TV was invented), and induced more than 1,000,000 to "hit the sawdust trail" as he called his tabernacle conversions. Using slangy language and reminiscing about his non-Christian baseball days, he was without peer in his time, and set a precedent for Aimee Semple McPherson, Oral Roberts, and Billy Graham, who followed him. The upper view is a capacity crowd gathered to hear him in the Sunday Tabernacle in the 1920s. Below, left, Homer Rodeheaver (almost equally well-known as his song leader), his sister Ruth Rodeheaver, and Mr. and Mrs. Sunday pose at a children's meeting at the lake in August 1931. At lower right are Billy, Bible under arm, and Mrs. Sunday at their Winona Lake cottage around 1910. Sunday died in 1935. (WLBC)

THE FRENCH LICK SPRINGS HOTEL, built in 1840 by Dr. William A. Bowles, gave Indiana its own spa and the famous Pluto Water which Dr. Bowles boiled, bottled, and sold as a tonic and a medicinal laxative throughout the country. A concentrated form of the mineral water was produced later in a plant *(above)* on the grounds of the hotel, which is in right rear. Visitors could drink the magic water for free in the pagoda, in right foreground. The namesake of the trademark, the Greek god Pluto, husband of Persephone and ruler of the Netherworld, graces the grounds of the hotel *(left)*. A particular attraction of the famous hotels was the waiters who carried their trays on their heads, using a special headgear *(below)*. This odd practice is still in use today. (Sheraton)

HISTORIC SAINT FRANCIS XAVIER CATHEDRAL at Vincennes in 1923: Construction started in 1827 on the site of an old French missionary church built in the early 1700s. At the graveyard in the rear are the unmarked resting places of French settlers and Indian converts who died more than two centuries ago. At left is the rectory, in the center, a building housing the magnificent library brought from France in about 1840 by the scholarly Bishop Simon Brute. (VU)

THE ORPHANS' HOME, as well as the Old Folks' Home (or Poor Farm) were standard institutions in Indiana in the 1920s when this picture was taken at the Pike County Orphans' Home near Petersburg. (ISL)

MANY RESIDENTS WELL-KNOWN in Fort Wayne are included in this photo of the English Lutheran Church building committee. The committee posed at the laying of the church's cornerstone on June 29, 1924. Standing, left to right: C. R. Wermuth, contractor; J. B. Franke; Al C. Wermuth; the Rev. Paul H. Krauss; Mrs. William Hahn; W. A. Bohn; Miss Bertha Krudap; Arnold Curdes; Miss Abbie Pfeiffer; J. W. Reynolds; George E. Becker; Gottlieb Heine; Adolph Foellinger; Nestor Fries; and Marshall Comincavish. Seated, left to right: E. C. Rurode; Miss Eliza Rudisill; Mrs. Carrie Heller; Mrs. Louise Bostick; Mrs. Sarah Wagner; Mrs. George Thompson; Mrs. E. F. Stiers; Mrs. Eliza Ogle; and Mrs. J. R. Meriwether. (FWPL)

PARROT PACKING COMPANY employees in front of the firm's sausage-making plant at Fort Wayne soon after the firm was founded in 1923. (FWHS)

PUPILS of Public School No. 30 in Indianapolis hard at work on their lessons in 1925. (ISL)

MILAN CENTER SCHOOL pupils relax from their studies for the "Story Hour" with their teacher. The "prayer bonnets" worn by several little girls in this Allen County classroom are traditional feminine headgear for the "plain people" of Pennsylvania-Dutch descent, such as the Amish, Mennonites, and Dunkards. (FWPL)

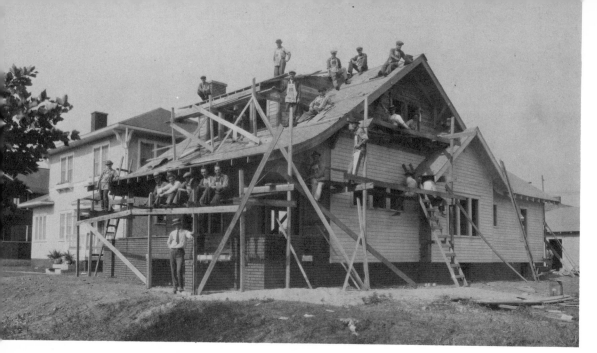

"LEARN BY DOING" was a principle applied at Indiana State Normal School, Terre Haute, in its industrial-arts class. Here, students get first-hand experience in building a house. (ISU)

MARVIN KUHNS, a native of Noble County, is said to have burned down the school he attended as a boy. It was replaced by this brick one-room structure, abandoned in the late 1920s. The juvenile delinquent became an early counterpart of desperado John Dillinger. After escaping from jail several times, he met his end in a horse-and-buggy gun battle with authorities and farmers near Van Wert, Ohio. The building that was once Stanley School is preserved in Kuhns' memory at the Chain o' Lakes State Park near Albion. (Adams)

THE KU KLUX KLAN, an old Dixie institution, was revived in
the 1920s with Hiram W. Evans of Atlanta at its head. It gained
great power and membership in many states, but nowhere more
than in Indiana. Under the leadership of a most remarkable
racketeer and organizer, D. C. Stephenson, it became a giant.
Stephenson revolted later when Evans tried to oust the former
Texan tramp printer for his immorality and high-handed methods.
He was said to have put $2,000,000 into his pocket in eighteen
months from his share of membership dues and "robe" sales.
This photo shows robed Klansmen forming a cross at funeral rites
for a fellow member in a small Indiana town. (ISL)

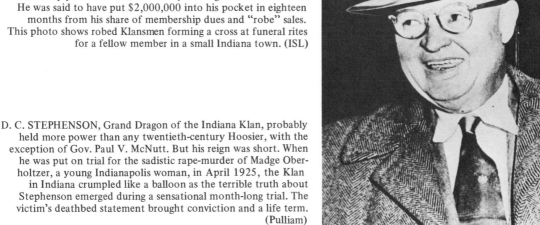

D. C. STEPHENSON, Grand Dragon of the Indiana Klan, probably
held more power than any twentieth-century Hoosier, with the
exception of Gov. Paul V. McNutt. But his reign was short. When
he was put on trial for the sadistic rape-murder of Madge Ober-
holtzer, a young Indianapolis woman, in April 1925, the Klan
in Indiana crumpled like a balloon as the terrible truth about
Stephenson emerged during a sensational month-long trial. The
victim's deathbed statement brought conviction and a life term.
(Pulliam)

ONE OF INDIANA'S most ambitious architectural projects was the creation of the five-block World War Memorial Plaza between Meridian and Pennsylvania streets in downtown Indianapolis. This picture is of the massed flags of American Legion posts from all over America at the cornerstone laying of the magnificent Memorial Hall, built of Indiana limestone, which dominates the plaza. Gen. John J. Pershing, commander of the A.E.F. in World War I, spoke at the occasion, July 4, 1927. (ISL)

CRIME WAS LESS RAMPANT than today on September 23, 1927, when America's sacred relic, the Liberty Bell, was displayed at the Indianapolis Traction Terminal. Only a single, determined Indianapolis policeman was deemed necessary to guard it from gangsters and vandals. The bell was on tour, by train, as part of the nation's 150th birthday celebration. (ISL)

GOV. HARRY G. LESLIE, seated, signs the bill levying taxes which made possible the erection of the Indiana State Library and Historical Society building at Ohio and Senate in Indianapolis. The structure was built of Indiana limestone. (ISL)

THE FRANCES SLOCUM MONUMENT at its original location in the family cemetery overlooking the Mississinewa River near Peoria, Miami County, was erected in 1900. It honors Frances Slocum, who, as "The White Rose of the Miamis," has been more romanticized than any Indian captive. Kidnapped in 1778 during the Wyoming Valley massacres in Pennsylvania at the age of five, she was discovered by a brother and sister at the age of fifty-nine, living as the wife of a minor Miami chief, the Deaf Man, near this spot. She refused to return with her kin, not willing to desert her Indian family and friends. The grave and monument have since been moved to another location across the river, to make way for the Mississinewa Reservoir.

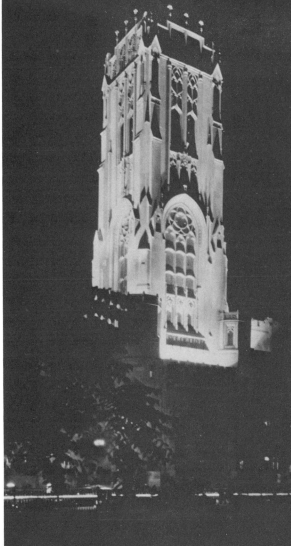

THE SCOTTISH RITE CATHEDRAL'S lighted tower just after its completion on North Meridian Street, Indianapolis, in 1930. (ISL)

[167]

MANY SMALL TOWNS improvised street fairs during the Depression years of the 1930s for the double purpose of providing entertainment and attracting business to the community. This is a scene in the principal business block on Branson Street at LaFontaine in the fall of 1929 or 1930.

THESE THREE REIGNING BEAUTIES rode a horse-drawn float in the LaFontaine Street Fair parade of 1929 or 1930. The sashes are somewhat misleading as the represented queens of the three Indiana metropolises were actually selected from among high-school girls of this small community.

ECONOMIC NECESSITY CAUSED many farmers to return to old-fashioned practices. Although generally used to burning coal in their stoves and furnaces, lack of cash made "buzzing wood" fashionable again. Fallen logs, limbs, and trees were hauled in and piled up in odd moments, and then neighbors gathered to "buzz" the piles with a tractor-driven circular saw. This scene is in Wabash County around 1930.

ENGLISH IVY was trained to form the university monogram on the wall of the Indiana University gymnasium. When the photo was taken in 1930, the institution at Bloomington had fewer than 4,000 resident students. Most of the campus buildings have been erected since. The student is from Elkhart.

TENNIS was for the few in 1930 when courts were available only at colleges and some municipal parks. This pretty devotee, in appropriate tennis garb of the day, is Lillian Spivey of Marianna, Arkansas, then a summer student at Indiana University.

THIS THREE-STORY BUILDING erected in 1878 and shown here in the 1930s was the principal structure at Vincennes University, the oldest institution of higher learning in the Old Northwest. It was razed in the 1950s when the university moved to a new location in Vincennes. (VU)

[169]

CUTTING DOWN THE NETS are the victorious Fort Wayne Central High School team members. The date of this photo is not certain, but the team was a regular contender for state honors in the late 1930s. (FWHS)

OUTSIDERS OFTEN EXPRESS DISbelief in newspaper accounts of the attendance at IHSAA state-tourney final games where Hinkle Fieldhouse at Butler University is usually filled to capacity, with thousands unable to obtain tickets. This picture of a tense moment should convince them! The tourney was moved from the "Cow Barn" on the Indiana State Fairground to the fieldhouse in 1928. (Schwomeyer)

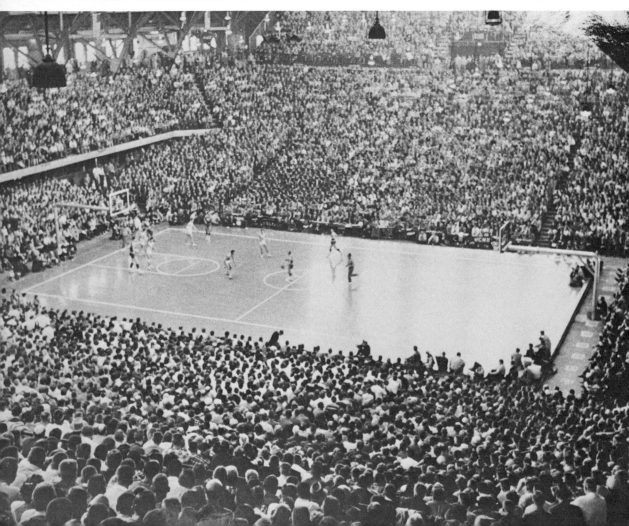

THE SMALLER SCHOOLS have always been "the people's choice" when the State Basketball Tournament finals were held—if they managed to survive to the finals. The crowds always hoped, usually vainly, that some small school would pull an upset. They were not disappointed in 1947, however, when underdog Shelbyville beat New Albany, with its sensational giant center, Clyde Lovellette, 68-58. Bill Garrett, second from right in rear row, set a new finals scoring record of 93 points. Coach Frank Barnes is in "civvies." (Schwomeyer)

NO ONE IN BASKETBALL has ever surpassed the combined playing and coaching record of Martinsville's Johnny Wooden, shown here in dribbling pose on the Purdue University floor. He played for Purdue from 1930 to 1932. Johnny led his high-school team to the Indiana High School finals at the "Cow Barn" each year from 1926 to 1928, and once to the state championship. He set a new all-time Big-Ten scoring record, and went on to coach UCLA to ten NCAA collegiate championships in twelve years! What a record! In the 1930s, shortly after this photo was taken, he coached Central High School at South Bend. (Purdue)

FRANKLIN HIGH SCHOOL became a legend as "Hoosier Hysteria" came into its own in the 1920s. Relatively small schools in Central Indiana began taking the state high-school championships regularly every year. Franklin, under Coach Griz Wagner, won "the state" three consecutive years, this being his 1922 team. Robert (Fuzzy) Vandivier, one of the all-time basketball greats, is on the left of the front row. He led most of the team to Franklin College, a tiny hometown school, and they dominated the national college picture just as they did the state. Other players are C. Friddle, Gant, Ross, King, Ballard, Williams, and Davis, with Coach Wagner at rear. (Schwomeyer)

THE FIRST U. S. SITDOWN STRIKE, a new and effective labor tactic developed by the U.A.W., newly affiliated with the C.I.O., occurred at the Bendix Automotive Products plant at South Bend in the early 1930s. The revolutionary but effective labor tactic, along with other U.A.W. incidents, provided national headlines that included a spread of several pages in *Life* magazine. Strikers' wives were much alarmed at published reports about non-union women supposedly smuggled into the plant as the union members locked themselves in. (NIHS)

AUBURN-CORD-DUESEN-berg, three names to conjure with among antique car buffs. The first two were manufactured at Auburn in the 1930s and the last, at Indianapolis. The Duesenberg was the most expensive American custom-made car of its time. Perhaps the fact that Indiana manufacturers concentrated on expensive, speedy cars and left the lower-priced mass-produced autos to Michigan firms explains why Indiana had only one auto manufacturer left by 1940—Studebaker. (Long)

THE STUTZ BEARCAT continued the great Indiana auto-making tradition into the 1930s. This roadster, a sensation for its speed and pickup, was a favorite with rum-runners as well as these two distinguished young men on the 1932 model's running board, who used it to inspect the outstanding high-school basketball teams of the state. They are William F. Fox, sports editor and basketball columnist for the *Indianapolis News*, and Paul D. (Tony) Hinkle, athletic director at Butler University. (Schwomeyer)

CAPT. EDDIE V. RICKENBACKER, pioneer auto racer and World War I aviation ace, bought the Indianapolis Motor Speedway track in 1927. Carl Fisher, the previous owner, had become preoccupied in his faltering development of Miami Beach. With Rickenbacker, right, is "Pop" Meyer, track manager. Rickenbacker built a golf course adjacent to the track in 1929, the year this shot was made. (Speedway)

INDIANA'S OWN WILBUR SHAW is being congratulated by Harvey Firestone, Jr., after winning the 500-mile race at the Speedway in 1931. He also won it in 1937 and 1939. There was never a more popular winner, nor a more lamented one, when he died after an airplane wreck. He is buried in the Vernon Cemetery in his native Wabash County. (Speedway)

[173]

THE "INDY 500" at the Indianapolis Motor Speedway on Memorial Day was well-established as America's best-known auto race in the 1930s. The track was much improved, but most spectators stood behind a protective fence at this start of the 1930 race. (Speedway)

COL. RICHARD LIEBER, German-born Indianapolis business-man, became the first director and leading spirit of the Indiana state park system when Gov. Samuel R. Ralston appointed a State Park Commission in 1915 for the State Sesquicentennial. Beginning by saving Turkey Run State Park and its fine forest from lumbering interests in a 1916 campaign, Lieber, portrayed here in 1944, built up the Indiana park system to a model for the entire nation during the 1920s. (ISL)

McCORMICK CREEK'S CANYON near Spencer, acquired in 1916, was the second unit of Indiana's state parks. In addition to a magnificent scenic gorge, the Inn and its adjacent swimming pool offered pleasant relaxation to visitors in 1932, despite the Depression. (Hohenberger)

HORSEBACK RIDING was popular with visitors of McCormick Creek's Canyon and Brown County
State Park. This is believed to be a scene at the latter in the early 1930s. (Hohenberger)

ELK IN INDIANA? These bulls were pictured dueling with their antlers in the early 1930s at Brown
County State Park, whose 15,000 acres provided ample room for a small zoo and a State-Department-
of-Conservation game farm. A small deer herd planted in the park gradually multiplied and spread out
until most counties of the state have deer now. (Hohenberger)

Facing page: SPRING MILL STATE PARK near Mitchell has several unusual attractions. One is Donaldson Cave, the opening of an underground stream, where visitors can take boat rides through a rock tunnel. The stream was famous in the late 1800s for its blind fish and the studies made of them by Dr. Carl Eigenmann, ichthyologist at Indiana University. In this 1930s scene, visitors view the remains of the flume used by the professor to carry water from the cave stream to the concrete ponds where he studied the tiny, sightless fish. (Hohenberger)

DORA COVERED BRIDGE, which carried a winding country road across the Salamonie River in Wabash County, and the wooded banks of the river presented a breathtakingly beautiful scene to shunpikers when the fall foliage turned color in the 1930s and 1940s. To make way for the Salamonie Reservoir, the bridge was moved to a site near Lincolnville, where it celebrated its one-hundredth birthday in 1974. (Hudson)

THIS LITTLE-KNOWN WATERFALL is in Pipe Creek in southern Cass County. It is one of the largest and prettiest in the state, with the original falls heightened by a shallow milldam built just above it.

FARMS HAD REPLACED the natural habitat of game in most of Indiana when this hunter sallied forth west of Indianapolis. Rabbits, squirrels, and imported pheasants were the principal game sought by hunters, who were able to get permission to search the stubblefields in the late 1930s. (ISL)

CONSERVATION OFFICERS gained more respect than the old-time game wardens in Indiana when the State Fish Hatchery was established at Lake Wawasee, the state's largest lake. Here game fish were hatched and fingerlings placed in the streams to replenish the supply. Shown with the department's truck are Heine Mosch and Tony Farley, in charge of the hatchery in the 1930s. (ISL)

GRASSYFORK FISH HATCHERIES near Martinsville was one of the world's largest growers of goldfish in the 1930s and 1940s, raising 50,000,000 fish a year in the springfed rearing ponds of its 1,500-acre farm.

COACH JAMES (JIMMY) PHELAN made Purdue University's Boilermakers one of the nation's top college football powers during the 1920s and 1930s. During that time, Purdue and Minnesota dominated the Big Ten. (Purdue)

NOTRE DAME AND ROCKNE were Hoosier names that dominated football in the twenties and early thirties as no other names before or since. Knute K. Rockne, Norwegian-born coach (with the bald head) is standing on the left in this picture of Notre Dame's 1924 National Champions. (Notre Dame)

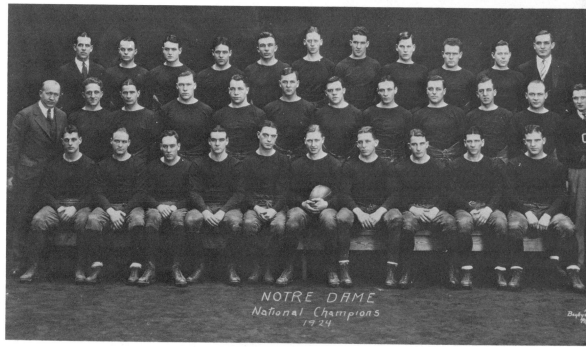

THE FOUR HORSEMEN of Notre Dame became a legend, along with their coach, Knute K. Rockne. They comprised the fleet-running backfield of the South Bend school's 1924 National Champions. From left to right are Crowley, Layden, Miller and Struhldreher. Elmer Layden came back to the school as its coach in the 1930s, after Rockne's death. He compiled an outstanding record on his own. (Notre Dame)

NOTRE DAME DU LAC received the last part of its name from the small lake on its campus. In the background is the university's famous golden dome, and the spire of the campus church. (Notre Dame)

[180]

PAUL V. McNUTT, white-haired ex-national commander of the American Legion and dean of the Indiana University Law School, probably wielded more power than any Indiana governor since statehood when he was swept into office in the Democratic landslide of 1933. He completely reorganized the state government into its present form. (Pulliam)

ROCHESTER, county seat of Fulton County, had a courthouse landmark familiar to many thousands of lake visitors and other travelers who passed it on US-31.

BANK ROBBER JOHN DILLINGER, "Public Enemy No. 1" on the FBI list during the early 1930s, made history when he posed for this picture with his shirt-sleeved arm on the shoulder of Lake County Prosecutor Robert Estill. The picture haunted Estill the rest of his life. A month later, on March 3, 1933, Dillinger broke out of Crown Point jail, using, he said, a wooden gun he had whittled. The outlaw, who had held up scores of banks and police stations, more or less became an Indiana legend and movie hero when an FBI squad mowed down in cold blood "the most brazen desperado since Jesse James" as he left a Chicago theater, one July night in 1934, with the notorious "Lady in Red." (Pulliam)

THIS IS ONE OF THE LAST survivors of the Indiana G.A.R., standing at the entrance of the Indiana Statehouse. (Hohenberger)

THE MADONNA OF THE TRAIL is this inspired monument honoring "pioneer mothers of covered wagon days." The famous statue, replicas of which mark other historic spots in each state on its route, was placed along US-40, on the east edge of Richmond, where the Old National Road entered the state. (Woodson)

MADONNA OF THE TRAIL

N·S·D·A· MEMORIAL
PIONEER MOTHERS
OF THE
COVERED WAGON DAYS

MONKS OF SAINT MEINRAD'S ARCHABBEY are shown observing Tenebrae Services at night during Holy Week. The Archabbey church has been remodeled since the photograph was taken by Brother Meinrad Kinder, O. S. B. The Benedictine monastery is one of the largest in the United States, with 180 monks and 400 seminary students. Founded in 1854, its Gregorian Choir is almost as well-known in Europe as in the United States. (SMA)

THE ABRAHAM LINCOLN Statue at Fort
Wayne is the only one depicting Lincoln in
his Indiana youth. Sculptor Paul Manship
included a book, Lincoln's ax, and his dog
to typify his pioneer childhood. Behind the
statue is the Lincoln National Life Insurance
Company building which houses the Lincoln
Library, said to be one of the largest collections in the world dealing with one man's
life.

BARR STREET FARMERS' MARKET in
1936 now had a tile roof to protect produce
and shoppers, and trucks had replaced wagons. (FWPL)

BREWERY OWNERS regarded fine draft horses almost as highly as Secretariat or Man-of-War, and retained them well into the century as prize symbols of the industry. This pair, in splendid harness, is drawing a Berghoff wagon at Fort Wayne. (FWPL)

MANY WORKING MOTHERS were the only breadwinners in the family in 1936, during the middle of the Depression. They left their children at day nurseries, where this picture was taken. (FWPL)

TROOP NO. 4, Boy Scouts, Fort Wayne, smartly stand at attention to salute the flag, even if not all the boys were uniformed—uniforms were hard to 'come by during Depression days. (FWPL)

LLOYD C. DOUGLAS, a Lutheran minister in North Manchester, was born in 1877 in Columbia City, where he spent his early life. He was the author of such best-selling religious novels as *The Magnificent Obsession, The Robe*, and *The Green Light*. The first two have each sold more than two million copies in hardback, a sale never approached by Tarkington and other popular novelists. Some of his books also became movie box office hits in the 1930s and 1940s. (Adams)

THE SOUTH BEND *News-Times* was a casualty of the Great Depression, suspending publication the day after Christmas 1937. Most Indiana county seats had two daily newspapers in the 1920s, but only one by 1940. Shown in 1937 are four key members of the editorial staff as they faced an afternoon deadline: Left to right, Horace Ward, Tom Philipson, Dan Mahoney, and Byron L. Troyer.

IN 1937 INDIANA bore the brunt of the most disastrous inland flood in the nation's history. The Ohio River cities were hardest hit in the flood which covered the entire Ohio-Mississippi length, drowning 400 persons, making a million homeless, and causing five hundred million dollars in damage. River cities unprotected by levees, as Evansville, were virtually inundated. This scene more than one mile from the normal river bank shows Bosse High School in Evansville, at the peak of the flood. (EVC)

THE FLOOD INVADED AURORA in late January 1937 and quiet reigned supreme over Main Street, the "main drag" of the city at the time. (Mrs. Thomas Miller)

DOWNTOWN EVANSVILLE is shown in this aerial view taken during the 1937 flood. The U-shaped building facing the water at the extreme left is the famous McCurdy Hotel, now a nursing home. Water was six feet deep in the lobby of the historic hostelry, which played host to many important people traveling by steamer as well as train. On January 30, the river crested at 53 feet, 9 inches above flood level, and covered nearly half the city. (EVC)

A VICTIM OF THE DEPRESSION was the *Vincennes Commercial*, whose business office is pictured as it was in 1920. Started in 1880, it was merged with the *Vincennes Sun* in 1930. Thomas H. Adams, standing at rear, was one of the editors who fought the Klan in the 1920s. (VU)

FARMERS along the Ohio River, many of whose ancestors came from Kentucky, produce the same flue-cured burley tobacco that the Kentucky Bluegrass Country is famed for. Here they apparently are getting a lesson in grading and preparation of "hands" from a Purdue Extension Agent. Burley was still being taken from such "hands" by many farmers in the 1930s and shredded for chewing or smoking at home. (Purdue Ag.)

FACTORIES SHUT DOWN by the score and industrial production slumped severely in Indiana during the Depression of the 1930s, but not farm production. Hoosier farmers produced more than ever before, and suffered disastrously low prices as a result. R. H. Hardin of Knightstown, shown husking his crop by hand, won the state corn-growing championship one year in the 1920s with a record measured yield of 129.7 bushels per acre. (Purdue Ag.)

A SOUTH BEND MAN, C. J. Morrison, was one of the first to use a honey-liquefying process so that he could sell honey by the bottle or can, instead of in comb sections as had been the practice. He is shown in his home-processing plant about 1937.

INDIANA'S STATE AND COUNTY FAIRS, since dominated by carnivals, were largely devoted in the 1930s to exhibits of the farmers' choicest products. This first-prize exhibit, representing all the farm crops grown in one county, was shown by James Spaugh of Bartholomew County at the Indiana State Fair in 1929. It represented hundreds of hours in preparation of choice specimens.

MORE THAN 100,000 FARMERS from all over the Corn Belt, a larger crowd than had ever witnessed a football game in America, were at Newtown, Indiana when this picture was taken. Here, on a fall day in the 1930s, part of the crowd awaits the start of the National Corn Husking Contest, the prime farm athletic competition. The white lines dividing the crowd are the "bangboards" of wagons belonging to state champions and runners-up of all the primary corn-growing states. Elmer G. Carlson *(right)*, twenty-six, of Audubon, Iowa, sets a new world record at the contest by husking 41.5 bushels of corn and throwing them into his wagon. That represented about 41,500 ears, and more than 120,000 motions in eighty minutes!

THE INDIANA STATE FAIRGROUNDS in northeast Indianapolis had but a single masonry building (the Coliseum) in 1916. Here, in 1926, the sheep have been honored with one, too, and Four-H Club boys exhibiting at the fair are relegated to the old frame sheep quarters, where straw-filled bunks have been installed for a boys' dormitory. State 4-H Club leaders and Purdue University Agricultural Extension personnel stayed with the country boys, and provided a week of interesting activities for them. The more-delicate girls had a masonry dormitory. The man with a coat, third row center, is Gov. Ed Jackson.

[191]

HARNESS HORSE RACING was dear to the hearts of Hoosiers, although there was no pari-mutuel betting, and few running races. Grand Circuit races, with such outstanding horses as Greyhound, Single G, and various members of the Directs line setting records there, were an annual event at the Indiana State Fair. Some of the nation's finest trotters and pacers also appeared on the half-mile tracks of the "Punkin Show Circuit," as the county-fair races were known. Here, a field of pacers are off to a fine, even start at an unidentified Indiana track in the early thirties.

AN INDIANA LIMESTONE QUARRY at Oolitic: This town, midway between Bloomington and Bedford, is in the center of the fine building-stone quarries by which Indiana has led the nation with production of limestone for decades. The name of the town comes from a stone known to geologists and others as oolitic, because of the tiny egg-shaped fossils which characterize it; other common names for it are Indiana limestone and Bedford stone. Many of the pretentious structures in America, as the Vanderbilt Mansion in North Carolina and stately offices, banks, and government buildings, are made of it.

CANYON INN, built in the tradition of the Old South, was a popular retreat from the turmoil of the cities in the 1930s and 1940s. It is located at McCormick's Creek State Park, near Spencer.

TURKEY RUN STATE PARK provided this inn for overnight visitors in a picturesque wooded setting that adjoins the gorge of Turkey Run in Parke County.

MOTORIZED SCHOOL BUSES had become the vogue for delivering country pupils to schools when this photo was taken about 1938 at Knox in Starke County. Pupils, drivers, and teachers pose with the equipment. (ISL)

"WORLD'S CORN KING," a title awarded at the International Hay & Grain Show during Thanksgiving Week each year, went to Indiana almost without saying during the 1920s and 1930s until the show was discontinued during World War II. This is C. E. Troyer of LaFontaine, who won the title in 1939. Both he and Peter J. Lux of Shelbyville won the title four times, more than any other corn growers. Other Indiana names on the championship roster behind him in the photo are: L. M. Vogler of Hope; Herbert C. Watson of Tipton; and William Carr Lentz of Jeffersonville.

WENDELL L. WILLKIE, from Rushville, was a rank amateur in politics and a relatively unknown utility executive. He created a sensation when he captured the Republican nomination for the presidency in 1940. His best-selling book *One World* advanced progressive ideas foreign to the G.O.P. leaders, but his down-to-earth homey Hoosier image appealed widely to voters. When he lost the election, he retired from political life to Rushville where seven farms and other interests awaited his attention. (Pulliam)

THEODORE DREISER, an Indiana boy, is shown interviewing members of poor families in Harlan, Kentucky, during a coal-mining dispute in the late 1930s. A stormy figure in literary and social movements, he was born in Terre Haute, lived in Sullivan, Evansville, Kosciusko County, and Bloomington before leaving Indiana. Few know that he could be conservative and sentimental, as when he wrote the words for "On the Banks of the Wabash." His brother, Paul Dresser, wrote only the music of the state song.

COKE WAS STILL A NICKEL before inflation ran rampant—as proven by this sign on Kentucky Avenue in Indianapolis in the late 1940s.

WHAT'S THE REASON FOR SHOWING a picture of this old post that the pretty little miss is leaning on? It's a very historic marker indicating the exact population center of the United States in 1940 near Carlisle, Indiana, officially determined by the United States Government. The marker was located in west-central Indiana for six previous decades, until Alaska was admitted to the union and upset the balance. (ISL)

WITH WORLD WAR II upcoming, it was prophetic when the Fort Wayne Civic Theater presented *Kiss the Boys Goodbye* in October 1939. Shown in an eye-catching episode are George Loegel and Rosemary Stanger. (FWPL)

WILLIAM DUDLEY PELLEY, a gifted novelist who became a rabble-rouser, was already in trouble with North Carolina authorities on charges of illegal securities sales when he moved with his printing press to Noblesville in 1940. An author of Hollywood movie scripts, he also founded a Nazi-counterpart, the Silver Shirts (disbanded by the Federal government) and a new religion, Soulcraft. For obstructing the American war effort, he was found guilty of sedition on August 6, 1942, and sent to prison. He died on July 1, 1965, after having been paroled. (Pulliam)

[197]

WORLD WAR II brought mobilization of the state's industrial plants, young soldiers, and citizens in an all-out effort following Pearl Harbor. Carole Lombard (nee Peters) of Fort Wayne, a leading movie star of the time, is shown on the Indiana Statehouse lawn on June 18, 1942. She had stopped in her home state for a rally during a nationwide Defense-Bond tour. With her, from left to right, are Henry F. Schricker, Governor Knox, Will H. Hays, Postmaster-General Sullivan, and Alex Arch of South Bend, who fired the first shot in World War I as a Yank sergeant. (ISL)

CAROLE LOMBARD poses in happier days on the lawn of her Fort Wayne home with her pet husky dogs. She and her husband Clark Gable probably were America's most glamorous couple at the time. In late 1942, she met a tragic death when the airliner in which she was returning to Hollywood crashed into the peak of Mount Charles, near Las Vegas, Nevada. (FWHS)

ELEANOR ROOSEVELT, wife of the late president, spoke in March 1941 at the dedication of the Union Building at Indiana State Teachers College. The institution at Terre Haute is now Indiana State University. (ISU)

MANY MILITARY training units were on Indiana college campuses during World War II after Pearl Harbor forced accelerated training of officers. This is a Navy V-12 unit at Indiana State Teachers College, Terre Haute, now Indiana State University. (ISU)

MANY CITIES along the line helped the historic Monon Railroad of Indiana celebrate its founding centennial in 1947. This scene shows residents of New Albany, where the initial tracks were laid in 1847, greeting the modern streamlined train at their station. One of the funniest train rides in American history was taken on this line by Horace Greeley, the famed New York editor, when he made the ninety-mile trip from Lafayette to LaPorte in nearly twenty-four hours. After traveling all night, mostly by handcar, he arrived exhausted at LaPorte, where he spoke on the evils of dram-taking. Like most Indiana independent railroads, primitive early service earned it a nickname, the "Moron Railroad," which has persisted until today. The Chicago, Richmond and Muncie (C. R. & M.) was known as the "Crooked, Rough and Muddy." (ISL)

A CHICAGO SOUTH-SHORE and South Bend electric train rounds a gentle curve at Meadowbrook in 1949. Advertising "Every Hour on the Hour," the line offered fast passenger service from South Bend, through the Calumet, to Chicago. News stories announced the suspension of service of "Indiana's last interurban" thirty-five years ago, but the "South Shore" continued to operate, meeting all the definitions of a local electric railway between cities.

BIG BARGES on the beautiful Ohio are in the front
yard of Hanover College, one of the oldest colleges
in the Midwest, founded in 1827. The students on
the bluff high above the river are enjoying the same
magnificent view which inspired Christopher Harrison, Indiana's first lieutenant governor, to choose
the post as a bachelor's hermitage after his fiancee
jilted this Virginia aristocrat for Napoleon
Bonaparte's brother. (Hanover)

PARKER AUDITORIUM at Hanover College is one
of the newer buildings on campus, and reflects much
of the quiet elegance of Virginia planter architecture.
(Woodson)

THE LIMBERLOST CABIN at Geneva was the home of novelist Gene Stratton-Porter until they drained her beloved Limberlost Swamp nearby. In 1893, she built this fourteen-room cedar log house at Sylvan Lake, now a much-visited state shrine. The photo was taken about 1948. Tree growth since then has changed the setting.

MAKING MAPLE SYRUP, although once common, is a dying industry on Indiana farms. In this Noble County woods, the syrup maker has replaced the pioneer's bucket with a plastic bag to catch the sweet sap.

THESE GRANT COUNTY Farm Bureau members mixed social activities with their meetings around 1949, as they executed the square-dance maneuver known as "diving for the oyster."

[202]

GREAT OLD WHITE ELMS were graceful features of Indiana landscapes until the 1950s, when the Dutch Elm disease hit the state, virtually wiping out the species in a few years. This Marshall County victim is being sawed into fire wood.

A NEWLY-FOALED SHETLAND PONY is proudly displayed in 1949 by a Wabash County farmer.

MRS. EARL S. WHITLOCK, a Miami County farm wife, prepares to take apples to the kitchen from storage in the family storm cellar in 1949. Many farms had such subterranean rooms near the house which doubled as a shelter during tornadoes and as a ground-cooled "root cellar."

[203]

EVERLY, INCORPORATED, one of the Midwest's largest livestock-hauling firms, shows off two rigs of its fleet which made a specialty of hauling hogs from northern Indiana to Pittsburgh packing plants. Located at Bourbon, the firm took over loads formerly hauled by the Pennsylvania Railroad. (Woodworth)

LIKE PEAS IN A POD—a thousand turkeys, and two little girls as well: The girls are Sandra and Sue, identical-twin, four-year-old daughters of Mr. and Mrs. John M. Howard of Fort Wayne. Most of the girls' flock of birds graced Thanksgiving tables in 1952.

A FARMER NEAR CONVERSE, seated near the ground, while his son drives the tractor, is shown ready to start setting tomato plants on his farm. When this photo was taken in 1950, Indiana, especially the north-central counties, led the nation in the production of tomatoes for canning and making catsup.

A FEW STERNWHEELERS were still operating in 1950 on the Ohio River. The *Charles Z., Jr.*, typical of the smaller steamers, is acting as a barge-pushing tug. (Lockridge)

MANY NATIVE HOOSIERS find fishing for channel catfish in the swifter waters of the state's streams just as exciting as angling far away in the Gulfstream or in Canadian waters. Enjoying the sport patiently in the 1940s is a Marion fisherman at a favorite spot, the fast water below the Charles Milldam in the Mississinewa River.

THREE AMISH CHILDREN from the vicinity of Middlebury visit Santa Claus at Deer Park, a nearby "storybook" resort in Michigan. They are far more interested in the photographer than Santa since Santa Claus is not a recognized institution of the Amish Christmas observance.

THIS "STORM KING" carriage of an Amish family is pictured in Nappanee, a popular trading city for the "plain people," who still use horses and buggies for transportation. Rollaway side curtains winterize the vehicle against icy blasts, and the horse's welfare is taken care of with a warm blanket.

The "energy crisis" of later years would be meaningless here, since there is plenty of oats, hay, and corn for the patient steed on the Amish farm.

THE FAMOUS AMISH "Barn Stars" are supposedly found only in two or three Pennsylvania counties. But here they are alongside State Road 4 just east of Goshen, in the heart of the Indiana Amish country. As the 1940s began, this structure was painted bright red and trimmed with white, presenting a pleasing landmark. Tourists are told that the stars are "hex" signs, designed to ward off werewolves, hobgoblins, and other evil spirits. Or is it just that the Amish love old decorative motifs brought back to Medieval Europe by Marco Polo from the Orient?

THE FORT WAYNE COMETS, shown here in 1949, introduced a new sport to the city, playing their at-home games in Coliseum. Always outstanding for the enthusiasm of its sports fans, Fort Wayne about this time had three ball teams in spring training in the South, as many as New York, including Brooklyn. These included the Zollner Pistons, national champions in softball, a national championship semi-pro baseball team, and a national women's championship baseball team. (FWHS)

TONY HULMAN, present owner of the Indianapolis Motor Speedway, holds the starting flag for the 1947 "Indy 500" race. (Speedway)

RIDE 'M COWBOY! Many Hoosiers enjoy a rodeo like the one put on at the Converse Fairgrounds by a touring show in 1950 with recent Western college champions providing the action.

SMITH WALBRIDGE CAMP for young people featured gymnastics in its summer program on a Kosciusko County lake during the 1950s.

A LAKE JAMES institution popular with summer vacationers in the late 1950s was the Lake James Christian Assembly, which owned the pier where these young members are sitting before going in for a dip. (Woodson)

HARRY S. TRUMAN, great old Democratic political campaigner, gave his last national political talk, and his only appearance in the Kennedy campaign for the presidency at Marion on Labor Day, 1960. He gave a rousing talk in typical Truman "give 'em hell" style, but did not mention candidate John F. Kennedy by name—not being fond of the Kennedys. Did this fool you? The man at the right is O. C. Worsley, a Marion resident, and amazing double for President Truman, being interviewed by Station WBAT's John Anderson in 1950.

[208]

COMMUNITY FAIRS PERSISTED in Indiana after World War II in many small towns, but the emphasis changed, with more stress on entertainment and less on farm-product competition. This is a high-school marching band in the parade at the street fair of New Haven in Allen County about 1952.

EASTERN HIGH SCHOOL'S STEL-larettes, a crack girls' drill team which was undefeated in three years competition, helped provide entertainment at many fairs and festivals in the 1950s, as here at the LaFontaine Street Fair.

THE FEW CIRCUSES that survive today are mostly domiciled in Florida, but the circus and carnival tradition lingers on with Hoosiers. These two Marshall County brothers pose proudly with their "baby doll" carnival stand.

THE FORT WAYNE civic theatre presented *Knickerbocker Holiday* at the Civic Theatre and later outdoors in Franke Park in 1949. At left are Ginny Maloley and Ann Cohen; third from right is Connie Weisman; and at right, Grace Drummon. Others in the chorus are unidentified. (FWPL)

THE FORT WAYNE Fortnightly Club was continuing a long-time social tradition when it met on January 23, 1950, at the home of Mr. and Mrs. John F. Brooks. The Brooks are greeting an arriving member, Mrs. William S. Mossman, at the door. (FWPL)

YOU STILL could get personal service in some independently owned supermarkets in the early 1950s. The proprietor of a Monon store waits on a customer during an apple promotion.

SORGHUM once provided much of the molasses used by Hoosiers, but is a rarity now. The gooey syrup with its own distinctive flavorings is still made in this authentic sorghum mill near Gnawbone in Brown County. Although the owners cater to tourists, both mill and product are authentic.

A RECENT GRADUATE of New Haven High School in Allen County finds a stack of corn shocks, with its accompanying pumpkin crop an appropriate place to carve her Hallowe'en jack-o-lantern in 1951. She later became Mrs. Robert Miller of New Haven.

PIONEER HI-BRED'S seed corn was grown in Tipton County for all its east-of-the Mississippi customers because of the excellent soil and climate there, particularly suited to corn-growing. Above is the company plant at Tipton, about 1951. A new plant was erected later at Rushville. Several hundred high-school boys from southern Indiana counties were recruited each summer by the company *(below)* to work in its Tipton County fields as detasseling hands. The hard physical work created super-appetites. A small part of the crew is shown in the chow line.

GRANT COUNTY 4-H Club members learn some fine points of pig judging on a farm near Fairmount about 1950. The two animals shown are good candidates for the title of "Miss Pig America."

SMALL-TOWN INDIANA has always nurtured companionship of a thoroughly democratic sort. Townspeople often catch up on the neighborhood news on cafe and drugstore stools. Here, salesmen, business people, and townspeople mingle at the sandwich bar of a Monon store in 1950.

LAKE CENTRAL AIRLINES was an Indiana-based line providing local service to many cities which did not have air transport otherwise. It was originally started and operated by Purdue University, but the government ruled this was not a proper function of an educational institution. The airline was sold to its employees, who purchased the stock. June Silverthorne, left, and Jacqueline Anderson are shown ready to start their regular flight schedules at Weir Cook Airport, Indianapolis, in 1953. Douglas DC-3s were standard equipment for the flights.

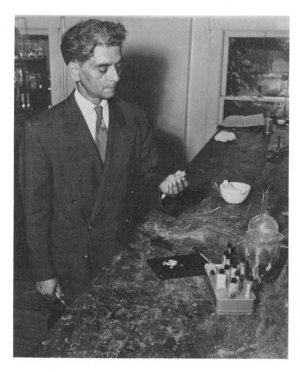

MANINDRA CHANDRA GUHA, a native of India, exhibits samples of the synthetic rice he invented in 1951 while a chemistry professor at Huntington College. Professor Guha also invented one of three rubber synthetics developed in World War II.

[213]

A DePAUW PROFESSOR and his class find the wooded campus more comfortable than the stuffy classroom in this late 1940 view at Greencastle. (DePauw)

ACADEMIC DIGNITY WAS cast aside when the DePauw University educators presented their annual "Faculty Follies" at Greencastle. The "backfield" plotting an intricate play in 1952 consisted of Joe Heston, Austin Sprague, Truman G. Yuncker, and Charles Bieber. (DePauw)

EPPLEY AUDITORIUM, gift of a donor to Culver Military Academy at Culver, has a theatre and other facilities unexcelled by many large cities. The campus and town are situated on one of the state's most beautiful assets, Lake Maxinkuckee. The academy's students have included princes, and the sons of movie stars and other celebrities.

FORDING STREAMS was common for buggies, wagons, and automobiles in southern Indiana well up into the twentieth century. But streams were mostly bridged when the picture was taken in the 1950s. Instead of traveling on a conventional bridge as it runs one trip a day to Corydon, the eight-mile Dinky Line Railroad uses a slab of concrete, laid in this stream bed. Corydon was once the state capital, and the battle of Corydon was fought here.

[215]

FERRIES across larger Indiana streams, once numerous, had virtually all been replaced by bridges by the 1950s. At Cannelton, however, this neat ferryboat connected people and cars with Hawesville, Kentucky, whose ferry dock and a few homes appear among the trees across the Ohio River.

IT WAS GRAND automobile nostalgia when Harold S. Vance *(left)* then president of the Studebaker Corporation of South Bend, met Charles Edison, exgovernor of New Jersey, at an auto show in the 1950s. They are seated in a 1902 Studebaker electric horseless carriage, the first auto model made by the firm. Edison recalled that he rode with his father, the famous inventor, in an identical Studebaker when he was a boy.

TWENTY YEARS TOO SOON: Studebaker Corporation pioneered the economical compact car with big gas mileage when it brought out the Studebaker Lark in the 1950s. It would have been handy in the days of the energy crisis.

[216]

INTERNATIONAL FRIENDSHIP GARdens, east of Michigan City, is a 100-acre memorial to world peace. Located in a small valley among the sand dunes, it features typical gardens of various nations. This group of visitors includes ex-Gov. Henry F. Schricker (extreme right).

THIS INDIAN patent-medicine man is demonstrating his product at the Auburn Street Fair in 1951. His eagle-plume war bonnet indicates that he is not a Miami but a "horse Indian" of the Great Plains. In his left hand is what he announces is a test tube of urine. His pitch is: "White man all the time get up nights. Indian no get up nights." For $1 a bottle, his Indian remedy will solve this paleface ailment.

[217]

TRINITY ENGLISH LUTHERAN CHURCH in Fort Wayne drew a large crowd to see its new edifice when the church was dedicated on September 17, 1956.

CATHEDRAL SQUARE of Fort Wayne is shown in this aerial view as mid-century approached. In the center is the Roman Catholic Cathedral of the Immaculate Conception. (FWHS)

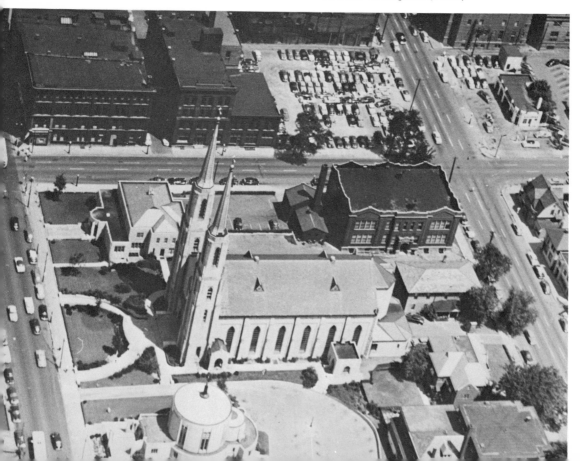

A MARIAN-YEAR CELEBRATION of the Roman Catholic diocese at Fort Wayne in 1954. (FWHS)

THE PEOPLE'S TRUST AND SAVINGS offices was a nineteenth-century building of special architectural interest in Fort Wayne. (FWHS)

THIS GIANT STATUE of Santa greets hundreds of thousands of children and their parents who visit Santa Claus, Indiana each year. The post office, where millions have sent letters to get the Christmas postmark, was renamed after the town, platted in 1846, found out that another town in the state had already appropriated the name Santa Fe. The Disney-type resort is in Spencer County, near Lincoln's boyhood home. (Koch)

AN OLD SPINNING WHEEL is operated at a twentieth-century Fort Wayne art festival by a pioneer, who remembered how yarn was spun in her youth.

PRESERVING HOOSIER heritage was the aim of the tiny town of Rockville when it organized the Park County Covered Bridge Festival in 1956. Scores of thousands came during the fall-foliage season to see exhibits of pioneer arts, and to take tours to the thirty-eight picturesque covered wooden bridges in the county. These Rockville women, in costumes from their grandmothers' day, are preparing bean chowder the old way for festival visitors. (Richter)

INDIANA BECAME IMPORTANT as another source of mineral wealth when the National Gypsum Company opened this nine million-dollar plant in the 1950s. Gypsum products for housing construction are mined here from an immense bed underlying an area near Shoals in Martin County. (National Gypsum)

THE NEW YORK CENTRAL installed what it claimed to be the most modern electronic sorting yard in the world at Elkhart in the late 1950s. This shows the electronic "brain" for the Robert R. Young yard. Alfred Perelman, who brought three railroads out of bankruptcy, was president at the time. The historic old road, as part of Penn-Central, has fallen on evil days again.

THE LAKE MICHIGAN SHORE and its inlets have long been favorite haunts of pleasure craft from the Midwest and elsewhere. This tiny schooner was out of Chicago in the 1950s. Storm warnings send most sailors scurrying for safe harbor because Lake Michigan can be as dangerous as the North Atlantic. Its storms have claimed hundreds of lives from the time of la Salle's *Griffon* to the present-day of coho-salmon fishermen in small boats.

THE FIRST ALL-BLACK TEAM to win the state basketball championship was the Crispus Attucks High School team of Indianapolis. The winning combination shown here achieved the title in 1955, defeating Gary Roosevelt High School 97-74, a new winners' and combined scoring record for a finals team. Oscar "Big O" Robertson, second from right in front row, scored 95 points in the two state-finals games. The coach (in sweater) was Ray Crowe. (Schwomeyer)

INDIANA CITIES were rapidly going suburban in the late 1940s and 1950s. This lovely home on Matter Park Road on the edge of Northwood subdivision outside of Marion was built by the proprietor of the Barley Fish Market.

THE NASHVILLE HOUSE, a local institution in Nashville dating back nearly to 1900, does an amount of business under its founder's son, Andy Rogers, that would be the envy of many a city enterprise. The atmosphere of the time when it was Nashville's only hotel is maintained in the store, where visitors can play checkers by the old pot-bellied stove. Behind the stove are enlarged photos of early Brown County life by Frank Hohenberger—and cartoons by Kin Hubbard (Abe Martin), which played a great part in publicizing Brown County. (Hohenberger)